MW00657549

HIGHER POWERED

DG 9/2016

HIGHER POWERED

A Ninety Day Guide to Serenity and Self-Esteem

JUDITH M. KNOWLTON

Edited by Rebecca D. Chaitin

Photographs by Gayle Burns

Continuum · New York

1991

The Continuum Publishing Company
370 Lexington Avenue, New York, NY 10017

Copyright © 1986 by Judith M. Knowlton

All rights reserved. No part of this book may be reproduced, stored in a retrieval system, or transmitted, in any form or by any means, electronic, mechanical, photocopying, recording, or otherwise, without the written permission of The Continuum Publishing Company.

Printed in the United States of America

Library of Congress Cataloging-in-Publication Data

Knowlton, Judith M.
[Listen to the action]
Higher powered : a ninety day guide to serenity and self esteem / Judith M. Knowlton ; edited by Rebecca D. Chaitin.
p. cm.
Originally published as: Listen to the action.
ISBN 0-8264-0542-8
1. Meditation. 2. Self-actualization (Psychology) 3. Self -respect. I. Chaitin, Rebecca D. II. Title.
BF637.M4K58 1991
158'.1—dc20 91–15510
CIP

For my daughter
CAROLINE FAITH HOBART

who knows all these things
. . . and so much more!

Contents

RAINBOWS

A friend has said of me that wherever I go I bring rainbows. What a wonderful compliment! Certainly my philosophy of life is rainbow-inspired. It is based on the consistent belief that good can come from evil, that positives spring from negatives just as the rainbow emerges from the storm. Oh yes, the sun's glory brings forth a prism of color, but without a myriad raindrops no rainbow is possible.

I have always thought and spoken in headlines, trite ones at that. Repeating the same slogans and sayings so often, I now have them thrown back at me when I least want to hear them. My friends seem eager to confront me with my own beliefs whenever I'm failing to live by them. My nature is relentlessly positive, and that's hard to stomach as a steady diet, even for me!

A few of these headlines may have originated with me, but most are borrowed truisms I use as a shorthand method of communicating my view of life. All of them have impact; they are memorable, powerful and motivating. Like life itself, they may at first seem paradoxical — but don't get hung up on seeming inconsistencies. *They are true!*

Some of these, my favorite sayings, may puzzle you, while others will not at first make sense. Focus on those you are most inclined to dismiss. They are the very ones that will make you *think*. Are you willing to open your mind to new ways of perceiving life? Take the ones you like, and leave the rest. But if you are at all like me, you may discover that the very ideas that disturb you the most are the ones you need to take to heart.

ACT AS IF...

THE 1st DAY

Perhaps you were told to buy this little book. Or did some caring friend present it to you with a cryptic note under your name on the gift page? "Because you're you." "A special gift to a special friend." Possibly you're skeptical about *any* "little" book. I don't blame you; I am, too. Are you much too intellectual to fall for the sentimental slop? Or are you so emotional that you seldom think things through, or just so world-weary that you can't be bothered?

This book will help you turn your attitude around, if you let it. I'm absolutely convinced that we *act* our way into new thinking and new attitudes. We do not, except with excruciating difficulty, *think* ourselves into new ways of *acting*.

Time for a transformation? Has someone you know made miraculous changes while you stand impotently by, wishing you could do the same? Then *act as if* the concepts in this book are true.

If it says, "Give yourself fifteen minutes of self-pity," then *do it*. If it says, "Expect miracles," then *start looking*. If it offers you a pristine white page on which to commit your attitudes and beliefs, then *write*! Even if you're blatantly anti-authority, as I am, and cannot stand being told what to do, just for the next few weeks *act as if you're teachable*!

(continued)

The plan of this book is to read one essay each day for ninety days, summarizing your thoughts at the end of each week on the page provided. The purpose is to approach your world, and yourself, in more positive ways.

The way to begin is to begin!

I will read one chapter each day at ________ o'clock in the ____________________.

Date ____________________

____

My signature

WHENEVER HE CLOSES ONE DOOR, HE OPENS ANOTHER

THE 2nd DAY

A friend brought a present for my new house, a stained glass piece that says, "God never shuts one door without opening another." I cried when I saw it; she knows my life has borne out that statement many times. I have come to a closing door, part of my life is ending, and suddenly an unexpected and *unforeseen* door bursts open in front of me with such force that I'm catapulted through.

That's not quite a true statement. I'm aware that I must *choose* to cross that threshold. If I make the decision to hang back and refuse, that particular door of opportunity and new life will slowly close, or even slam shut. But if I'm watchful and expect another door to appear — if I trust Him — it will soon be there, beckoning and welcoming, and my life will ascend to a new level.

Through fear or rigidity or self-will, I can refuse to step through every single door that opens before me. Then life will remain static, dull, purposeless and "safe" — always with the implied question, "Is this all there is?" But I know there is more; I need only be willing to accept it when it's offered.

I watched as my exasperating, delightful, vital husband, Len, slowly melted away from me with cancer. As a new widow at 50, I understood that I would survive physically (people do!) but at four o'clock every morning I woke to the reality of my empty bed. (Those two words are the symbol of agony!) Sliding into purposelessness and depression, I didn't give a damn what happened to me. When the anguish became too great, I asked my Higher Power what to do at this early hour — alone in bed — to help me survive. The answer was immediate: *write.*

I was not a writer. But for several years I'd wanted to put a couple of concepts on paper. Now was surely the time and opportunity. I had always known that the way to become a writer was to write, so I did that — every morning. Piles of crumpled-up rejects flew from my bed. It was not fun! A friend whose husband had died suddenly just a couple of months earlier — a professional editor — began to work with me. We wrote, talked, passed drafts around, and at last became co-authors of two tiny books, *Detachment* and *Enabling.* In a very real sense, our husbands caused those books to happen.

I believed no one would print "D&E" as I visualized them, little gift books to cherish. So I designed the covers, discovered a typesetter, chose typeface, paper and colored inks, found printer and binder. Everything I needed fell into place whenever I asked the single question, "Where do I find...?" I turned QUOTIDIAN, my husband's alcoholism counseling corporation, into a publishing company. My distributor is an old friend who was already doing business in alcoholism and personal growth books. Through him I made contact with the author of *This New Day,* and I was launched as a publisher. I didn't launch myself. I was willingly catapulted into a new life of opportunity and creativity far beyond anything I could imagine for myself.

You're holding this book in your hands now because one door swung shut and another swung open and I was able to say to myself, "It's *got* to be better on the other side than where I am right now!"

ONE DAY AT A TIME

THE 3rd DAY

I am continually impressed, even astonished, by the depth and meaning inherent in the phrase, "Live one day at a time." My grandmother often said to me, "I live each day as it comes," and she was healthy and alert until her death at ninety-four. The Bible says it this way, "This is the day which the Lord hath made; we shall rejoice and be glad in it."

The profundity of this concept lies in the inescapable fact that it is right, it is life-enhancing, it is simple to understand — and so difficult to carry out! I have directed far too much of my thought, time and energy to the errors and humiliations of my past. I've expended even more time, energy and thought on fears and expectations for the future, and on dreams that may not come true — and would be enormously damaging to me if they did.

People say that "one day at a time" is like bank transactions:

Yesterday is a cancelled check;
Tomorrow is a promissory note;
Today is cash in hand; spend it wisely.

That's well put, don't you think? Understandable and clever? But I stutter over it, because I'm not knowledgeable about promissory notes and keep forgetting the words. I'm much more in tune with a visual concept that no one ever forgets, especially when a grey-haired lady (me) comes out with it:

If you have one foot in yesterday
And one foot in tomorrow,
You're going to piss all over today.

Now *that's* unforgettable.

NOTES

THE 4th DAY

I'm an alcoholic. This means alcohol was my great friend for many years until it backfired on me. I used it for fun and fear, sex and socializing — and everything in between. Slowly it did my mind in; at the end I was keeping company with a talking bathtub (hallucinations are often creative!).

I embraced alcohol precisely because I wanted the most out of life, to get that glorious warm feeling and the highest high. Compulsion and I have had a long history. I quit smoking years ago, leaving me with three active addictions: sugar, caffeine and auctions. Don't laugh! All are surprisingly insidious and powerful. I ask myself, how can I possibly give up my morning coffee? That's addiction whispering. And I go on sugar binges. Sugar's a potent mood-altering drug for me: euphoria followed by anxiety, depression and even paranoia can be part of that sweet package. Withdrawal from sugar can sometimes mean five days of acute discomfort — and I don't want to give up *any* immediate comfort for some distant good. That's addiction talking too. Gambling of all kinds (auctions, bingo, lottery, cards or dice) can be the root of more euphoria and inner turmoil. Addiction is an all-consuming passion.

I'd better get to the point. Here's my pitch: I challenge you to be chemically free and compulsion-clean during the ninety days that you're absorbing the ideas in this book. (I'll spot you nicotine and caffeine, because I'm not a complete monster or that pure, myself!) You simply don't take the *first* snort, puff, pop, drop, sniff, shot, taste or bet. I'm not up on all the terms, but no looking for loopholes. You get my meaning. And look to your stash of doctor-dealt tranquilizers. They're part of the problem.

If you stay "clean" without difficulty, that's terrific. But I can assure you that it's not so easy to be straight and sober in the U.S.A. today; there's an awful lot of pressure to conform. Whether or not you're truly dependent on something, these ninety days will give you a whole new perspective on mood-altering substances.* If you make this commitment to yourself, and then find you're unable to stick to it, find someone to talk with: a friend who's in one of the self-help programs, or a counseling service in the yellow pages under "Substance Abuse" or "Alcoholism." They've got the knowledge and experience.

Getting high on life alone is a hard concept to accept until you've been on this side of the mountain. Over here it feels marvelous, but you've got to experience it to make an educated choice. After three months clean, you'll have a knowledge of both sides. Then you can *choose* to stay sober, or go back to your drug of choice. As recovering people like to say, "We'll be glad to refund your misery."

---

*If, as you read this, your mind kept pooh-poohing the whole idea, take another look at your behavior. Addiction blows so seductively in your ear!

Bloom Where You're Planted

THE 5th DAY

The first time I saw a poster with this phrase, I did a double-take. It started me thinking of all the "When I. . ." statements I'd run through my own head, or heard others say:

I have dreams and goals, so. . .
When the kids are grown I'm going to. . .
When I get the new job I can. . .
When I get my degree. . .
When I move to a bigger house. . .
When I marry the perfect. . .
When I win the lottery. . .

then all these wonderful dreams — which I'm putting no effort into right now — can (magically?) come true!

But then a niggling voice in the back of my head says, "What if the *when* doesn't happen? Then what?"

I imagine this healthy little plant in a simple terracotta pot, basking in the sun in front of a flower shop. No flower yet — not even a bud — but no ordinary plant, this. It has *ambition*! It dreams of blooming in the White House Rose Garden. Laudable! And it has only a couple of limitations to deal with: the flower shop is in Kansas, and the plant is a geranium. No matter. It will store up the glory of its bloom until that marvelous moment when it achieves its goal in life!

Along comes a little old lady who loves flowers. She admires the healthy plant and sees all its potential for beauty. Home she goes with it for her front step, where she knows it will add charm and color — *as soon as it blooms*.

Too late the unbudded geranium learns that the President's motorcade is coming right past its pot this very afternoon. No way can it produce a spectacular blossom in time to be recognized and applauded. No one ever told it there's one helluva difference between potential and performance!

NOTES

Change Is The Only Constant

THE 6th DAY

Time was when I didn't know that! I used to work so hard getting my daily life into good order. I'd settle into a routine that became increasingly comfortable: talking with friends, going to church, planning weekend entertainment, taking care of the family, getting on with my education . . . and then *wham*! My well-orchestrated life would fall apart again.

A special friend would move away, someone would have an accident, there'd be a death in the family, the car would need major repair, the washer would break down — things like that. And my comfortable, constant routine was again a shambles! Every few months another upheaval. I blamed myself for not managing things better. Why else was my perfect life going awry?

Where did I get the misguided idea that if I did things *right*, my little world would be forever smooth and calm? Nothing could be more unrealistic or further from the truth. What I *can* expect is change: constantly, repetitiously, continuously. This is neither bad nor good; it simply *is*. Change is life; life is change. Oh sure, I know this intellectually, but am I still secretly doing battle in my heart?

I discovered that I always have choices, and sometimes it's only a choice of attitude. I can dread the unexpected and hide from life by closing doors and protecting myself from who knows what. Or I can wake up each morning in anticipation. And so I do! My life isn't falling apart; it's moving on. Ever an adventure. What surprise awaits me today? Will it be humdrum or unusual, ecstatic or tragic or sad? I cannot know. The mystery will unfold for me.

With this attitude, as a friend likes to say, "My life is uncommonly good."

Does my attitude make it so? I believe it does, because I'm now willing to embrace life on life's terms. It needn't go "my way" but I'll still accept it. Oh, not all the time, of course! I'm merely human, though I hate to admit it. So I'm overcome with grief for people gone too soon, or enraged by injustice. But I do what I can, and the feelings pass, taking their place in the history of my life. All is well.

NOTES

Living In The Now

The 7th Day

After I stopped my alcoholic drinking, I began to reconstruct my life. Up to that time, I had no idea that I could gain control over the maneuvers and meanderings of my mind. I knew my formal education had put certain facts and theories into my brain, but I believed other ideas just appeared there somehow, unbidden. My mind rushed into the past or flew into the future without plan or purpose — a free-association kind of thing that could be interesting and creative but wasn't directed in any positive, productive way. Even when I made an effort to remain in the present, I was unable to keep my attention focused. I finally understood the concept of living "one day at a time," but I needed to teach myself how to live in the present moment, realizing instinctively that it would take enormous effort and concentration and constant practice.

Sunday sermontime at church seemed the ideal time and place to begin. My minister will forgive me. He's an excellent preacher, but while he was speaking, my mind was forever drifting away to my work, my dreams, my family or my preparations for Sunday dinner. No matter what the subject, I was never "here and now," so I decided to focus all my energy on the twenty-minute sermon. There I was, listening without interruptions to a dynamic speaker — and I was absolutely unable to do it. My mind was unmanageable! Every two to five seconds I drifted out the stained glass window into some other world. I hauled my mind back to the pulpit over and over and *over*. It was exhausting. By the end of those few minutes I was frazzled and had begun to understand what people mean when they say that changing yourself is hard work.

I became increasingly fascinated by the haphazard functioning of my brain. Once I was aware of the whirl of thoughts, I became more skillful at controlling them. Awareness expanded. I was able to pay more attention to *all* my senses: the subtle noises, odors on the air, the touch and taste and feel of my world. I graduated to ten-second increments of "now" before my concentration broke.

I listened to family and friends and even total strangers, perhaps for the first time in my life. I looked into their eyes; I noticed nuances of expression. I responded to people instead of simply playing out my own expectations. The shell of my protective ego began to soften. It was wonderful and stimulating and I recognized it for what it was — I was getting high on life!

It's been several years since I began to practice living in the present. I'm now able to sustain myself *in this very moment* a good deal of the time, though I slip back whenever I'm not vigilant. My thinking is now *decisional.* What I mean is, if I want to examine the past, it's no longer an unexpected experience. I also make a decision to daydream, fantasize, brainstorm and make future appointments. Friendships have become more precious as I experience them *now*; there's a sense of urgency, because this person may never touch my life again. There are no guarantees for tomorrow. And my mind is clearer, more focused and disciplined. It's been well worth the constant effort.

An interesting benefit is that in the present I have no fear or apprehension, because my mind simply has no room for them. This practice has granted me many moments of serenity, and I'm sometimes stabbingly conscious of what I understand to be God's will for me. Curiously, I learn this by remaining in the present, *not* by praying about the future. Do I no longer fear death because I no longer avoid life? Perhaps. When I'm living in this moment I have no need to question.

WHAT IS MY ATTITUDE TOWARD TAKING ACTION, LIVING IN THE NOW, MAKING A COMMITMENT, STAYING CLEAN AND SOBER?

POSITIVE PEOPLE

THE 8th DAY

I always feel better when I'm around certain people. I feel more alive, more worthwhile, more certain that life has purpose and meaning through my contact with them. They are special.

They're willing to listen to my troubles, but not for too long. They keep tragedy and joy in perspective.

They're open to new ideas, and get excited about mine.

They're childlike, having time for fun and games. They laugh easily, and cry easily too.

They're spiritual, knowing without being preachy that a Higher Power guides their lives.

They're responsible, doing the things they say they'll do, and on time. They can be trusted.

They're tolerant of me, giving truthful evaluation and criticism lovingly and gently, but firmly.

They are not gossips.

They're self-respecting, caring first and foremost for their own mental and physical health. They avoid things that may harm them, and know when to say "no."

They're committed to positive change and always have time to savor simple beauty.

Lately I find myself practically *running* from negative, judgmental people. I want only to surround myself with energizing, positive ones. But there are very few who've gotten so far on their spiritual journey. What to do when I find myself with someone who's down, depressed, unsure and hesitant? I take another look. Usually that person has a glimmer of faith, just the faintest idea that change is possible, a willingness to look for new ways. That's positive enough for me!

I'm energized by that flicker of willingness, because I believe a miracle is in the making. A new person is about to bloom; it's the simple willingness that does it. Then I begin to think of myself as a catalyst for change; I may be able to help fan that spark as other positive people have fanned the spark in me. It works just that way.

NOTES

ACTIONS CHANGE ATTITUDES

THE 9th DAY

There are a number of things I don't care for in my personality. I've developed very strong opinions and attitudes without even recognizing my feelings. Over my lifetime I've become rigid in all three areas. Push my button and I respond predictably. I don't like that. It presumes a total lack of personal growth. Starting now, I'm committed to changing myself.

My attitudes are my most rock-solid feature, ingrained from early childhood. It's been said that our attitudes die an hour after we do, and I believe it!

My beliefs (that is, thoughts, opinions and prejudices) have been polished over years of personal experience, observation and formal education.

My feelings follow automatically, as if they were engraved in stone. How in heaven's name will I go about changing any part of me?

I've just become a grandmother. She's an adorable child, but I just don't like babies. I feel awkward and uncomfortable and would rather keep my distance, even though I've had three children of my own. I feel guilty; isn't baby-cooing instinctive for all women? Well, it isn't! So I share my discomfort with friends and find that several of them have the same attitude. Up to now they've avoided admitting it out loud. What's the next step? I hold the baby!

No, I'm not trying to be funny or cute. Changing a deeply ingrained attitude, feeling or belief is difficult — almost impossible. Changing an *action* is relatively easy. The surprise and pleasure of it all is that once the action is changed, thoughts, attitudes and feelings *all change as a result!* So I need only ask myself how I wish to *behave* in a given situation. The rest will follow.

It just takes practice — a lifetime of practice!

NOTES

Cinderella's Slipper Is A Size Three

The 10th Day

. . . and Peter Pan's little suède boot is a size four! Just look at your own feet. That's not you! Playing sweet little innocent child doesn't get good reviews any more. It isn't cute. In fact, it's downright embarrassing to watch.

I'm a counselor by profession, and many people come to me in all stages of perplexity and frustration, most often because their marriages are disastrous. Their spouses (or parents or children) are alcoholic, and they've been beaten down emotionally. They've used every maneuver and manipulation in the book to get the alcoholic to straighten up while they remain innocent of any mistake. Of course nothing has worked, and the maneuvers have been exhausting. I give them verbal kicks in the ass — just the things you're finding in this book — and I give homework, self-focusing actions that take expectations off the "souse." In no time at all my clients have stopped looking for a shining prince or Mama Wendy.

The changes are miraculous. A forty-year-old woman stops looking out from under coyly lowered lashes; her prissy, whiney little voice drops an octave. She even stops dressing in little-girl ruffles. A fify-year-old man gives up slouching defiantly in his chair like a belligerent teenager. All of a sudden they stop manipulating and start becoming self-responsible adults.

I know how it feels to make this transition into adulthood. When I did it, my body noticeably shifted gears. My head came up. No more hunched shoulders and furrowed eyebrows. I didn't wheedle any more, so my voice went from sickly supplicating to firmly factual. My throat relaxed. It didn't happen overnight, but it did happen once I took the focus off Prince Charming. When I became responsible for myself first, the need to maneuver disappeared. The helpless little kid pleading with Daddy flew out the window. I never want to go back there; it was too unattractive a role. And if I find myself reverting even a little, I say to myself, "Size three, huh? Forget it. I'm a seven."

NOTES

FORGET ABOUT FEAR

THE 11th DAY

I grew up believing that sensations like a pounding heart, a squeeze in the gut and a rush of adrenaline signaled a positive feeling of anticipation, not dread. So I have litte patience with myself when I invoke fear, because for me it's apt to be an excuse-laden, immobilizing reaction. Caught in some business or emotional risk, for example, I find myself plaintively wailing, "But I'm *afraid*!" "Good heavens, so what?" I rebuke myself. "Is fear a good enough reason to avoid intelligent action? No way!"

Thoughts or perceptions come first. Feelings are the result of that first thought, so it follows that a particular feeling in a particular circumstance is by no means inevitable. *I can change my perception (thought) and therefore the feeling.* I'm not talking about the anguish in the bowels and slam to the heart when an eighteen-wheeler hurtles toward me out of control. The preceding vision and noise register "Danger!" even if I don't have time to verbalize a conscious thought. I don't want to become hardened to that kind of perception, because I need the flood of adrenaline to get me moving before I'm mincemeat.

On the other hand, faced with a social or business risk, my thinking goes something like this: "I don't want to look foolish; I don't want to fail; I don't want to be rejected." Put that specifically, it's more manageable than simply pleading fear, because I'm acknowledging to myself that I'm really saying, "I refuse to take action."

At last I found a solution to all these mental gymnastics. I learned to be more honest with myself, replacing "I'm afraid" with "I'm paralyzed," because that's what I was really telling myself. Then I got immediately angry. "No,

I'm not! That's not true!" Instantly I felt myself letting go of those powerful, paralyzing words, "I'm afraid." Instead I was able to admit to being anxious. "Anxious" is honest, but not immobilizing! Once I modified the thought, the feeling was modified too. That's the way it is with feelings. It left me free to act.

And if, for some reason, the fear stays with me, I can still make a rational decision and say to myself, "Okay, but I'm taking the risk regardless."

NOTES

No Need For Courage

THE 12th DAY

Do you have trouble with serious decision-making? Do you vacillate, so unsure of the best action to take that you end up doing nothing, convinced you haven't the courage to act?

I've learned a most interesting fact: *you don't need courage*! Courage comes later. If I'm sitting in my room, face contorted as I attempt to "screw my courage to the sticking point," all I've done is stave off the action. I've also raised my anxiety level and fogged my brain with "what ifs." That's not accomplishing much!

The steps to acquiring courage go something like this:

1. Concentrate on the problem and get all the facts.
2. Consider available alternatives.
3. Brainstorm these alternatives with action-oriented friends and solicit their ongoing support.
4. Make an informed decision.
5. Take action.

What is so astonishing about these five steps is that when I concentrate my energies where they belong — on solving the problem — I lower my anxiety level because I don't feel helpless. I become more educated and objective about the problem, and accomplish the necessary goal. *Now* I can look back and say, "That took courage!" But it didn't, you see — it simply took *action*!

If you're not sure about this, listen to an interview with a hero who's just performed a courageous feat. He usually says something like, "I just saw what had to be done, and I did it." No working up courage. No Tarzan yodel through the jungle. Just an action. A courageous *action*.

After you've taken action, you'll agree with me. It only sounds like nonsense until you've experienced it!

NOTES

What Other People Think Of Me Is None Of My Business

THE
13 *th* *DAY*

I grew up in an emotionally controlled family. Seldom were there raised voices, let alone fights. One particularly hot evening, however, my parents began shouting at each other. But first they ordered my little brother and me to close up the house so the neighbors wouldn't hear. I can see it as if it were yesterday: my six-year-old brother running for the front door, palms pressed forward and arms braced, to slam it shut. It all made a great impression on me; evidently what the neighbors thought of us was enormously important.

Another frequent message I received was, "It isn't done" — presumably by "good girls." I could never figure out how my mother knew *it wasn't done*! With these two basic messages burned into my brain, I spent years feeling agonized in social situations, trying to keep a proper middle road and failing miserably. I'm so rebellious that I still tuck my feet under me when I'm sitting, just to show my mother — who's been dead 25 years — that I can put my feet on the furniture if I want to.

I like the title of this chapter, because it's blunt and to the point. It also implies that what *I* think of me is my business indeed. I need to answer to myself, to be self-responsible, because I'm focusing clearly on my own values and standards. It's not my business what "they" think, because I don't base my behavior on their opinions, but on my own. Of course this is not a hundred-percent attitude. Valued friends' opinions *do* count; I frequently need outside verification and validation. But basing my decisions on me and not "them" is a dramatic shift in my approach to life. Social anxiety is reduced to practically nothing (at last!) and my life is now pretty consistently satisfying.

This is no new concept. The last generation — and several generations before them, because I'm quoting Shakespeare — said the same thing in more eloquent language:

"This above all: to thine own self be true."

NOTES

GO WITH THE FLOW

THE **14th** DAY

I've heard that phrase so often. I once thought it meant: Don't go against society, don't be original, don't stand out from the crowd, don't fight City Hall. But I've always been a rebel and a battler for causes; "Go with the flow" sounded like abject passivity. I was against it.

Let me tell you how I found the Old Stone House, whose peaceful pictures enhance this book. I've known since the age of ten or twelve what my dream house would look like: a centuries-old stone house nestled into the side of a hill, with wide floorboards, beamed ceilings and a walk-in fireplace with a hanging kettle. Upstairs, the huge loft would be my bedroom. The pond would have a little island to shelter the ducks and geese. That's it, always the same — my house.

Months after my husband died, my house began to come to mind again. I even went so far as to visit a couple of real estate offices. They didn't exactly laugh at me when I told them about my house, but they assured me I was looking for a rare find indeed, and I wouldn't be able to afford it if perchance I came upon it! But I stubbornly continued my search. One day a friend and I took a drive through the Pocono Mountains. We looked at houses with an agent, but found nothing of interest, so on the way home I suggested several meandering turns onto country roads. Gradually I became aware that my house was nearby. I know that sounds like fantasy, but it's true. As we rounded a curve I remarked calmly, "There's my house." A moment later the "For Sale" sign came into view.

The next day I visited the Old Stone House with an agent. We strolled by the pond and admired the charm of the house from a distance, while the geese eyed us from their island. I had no feeling of trespassing; I knew I was surveying my own land. My experience of the place continued to be strange and wonderful: as I stepped past the heavy plank door I was enveloped in tranquility. The loft room was as big as I'd pictured it, the fireplace as wide and welcoming. I embraced the serenity of "home."

The following week my brother and I visited the place together. He was entranced with it too, and we daydreamed of building his little retirement home somewhere on the property. Later I learned he'd told several friends, "I wish I could just write a check for my sister to buy her house." Three months later, in a tragic way, he did — by dying an agonizingly unexpected death and leaving me his own house, with enough equity to buy mine. I was profoundly shocked by the experience — my gain from my loss. Overwhelming sadness. Yet it felt *right* at the same time. I can't explain it any better.

What does "Go with the flow" have to do with buying my house? Everything. I kept saying to myself, "I can't, it's too soon, it's too much, it's too far, it's too big. To buy the house so close on the heels of my brother's death would be terribly wrong." Then the agent called to inform me that another purchaser had showed up. I simply could not put this thing off. I saw my life veering in an uncharted direction out of my control, but I also had the uncanny sense that things were unfolding as they were supposed to.

Going with the flow has that "supposed to be" quality. It is action-oriented and self-actualizing. There's nothing passive about it. In fact, I may have to paddle like hell to stay in my own current. I know my little stream may take a sharp plunge over steep rapids at any moment, while everyone else is floating down the lazy river, but unexpected "coincidences" will ease my way through the back eddies. If I stray from my own stream and buck fate, I know it immediately because I slam up against rocks and shoals and nothing works. (When a couple made an offer on the house the very same day, the owners rejected it in favor of mine. Somehow I knew that would happen; my life was moving inexorably in that direction.)

When I'm going with the flow of my life, the sense of

rightness and purposefulness and guidance are startling. The core of my being seems to remain calm; doubts are minimal. Tremendously hard work may be necessary, but it's exhilarating, never exhausting. That's one of the ways I can tell it's right for me. I know you've had the feeling too. You may remark in wonder, "Why, I'm on a roll," or you may simply recognize you're marching to the powerful beat of a different drummer. But I also know that many people fight against their own flow, digging deep canals in an attempt to change direction. When they're exhausted from the struggle, their motto becomes, "Life's a bitch, and then you die."

Once upon a time that was my sad old motto, too. No longer. Going with the flow of my life, not knowing what's around the next bend, not needing a map, fills me with contentment, joy and serenity, like coming home to the Old Stone House.

H.A.L.T.

THE 15th DAY

I'm an outrageously compulsive person, an extremist who seems to have only two speeds: full tilt and full stop! I need short-cut slogans to slow me down on my headlong flights. Simply repeating the mind-stopper, "H.A.L.T.!" gets me to re-evaluate my behavior, usually none too soon. The admonition is clear; I must avoid becoming too Hungry, Angry, Lonely or Tired. Any one of these results in irrational thinking, poor decision-making and emotional binges (the "stinking thinking" that used to get me into so much trouble).

Too hungry. When I fail to eat with consistency and care, I become irritable and waspish. Trying to correct this, I resort to sugar binges that often throw me into an emotional tailspin — at first euphoric, then angry, depressed and self-pitying.

Too angry. When I stop taking my own character inventory regularly, when I avoid expressing my hurt (with me, hurt is usually the flicker of feeling that precedes anger, and I've always admitted more easily to anger than to the vulnerability of hurt), then my irrationality grows and I slide into outright alienation.

Too lonely. My thinking is as clear, honest and realistic as the degree of contact I have with friends and acquaintances. Separation from my support system leads to further withdrawal. More important, it can lead to the conclusion that I don't need anyone else — that I'm emotionally self-sufficient. Dangerous belief!

Too tired. Once I become mentally or physically exhausted, I begin to make serious mistakes in judgment. Perception of my world shifts to that ominous three-in-the-morning anxiety and I lose all gratitude and positive outlook.

"H.A.L.T." gives me that little flag of warning, the awareness I need to haul myself back to self-caring and realistic behavior before I plunge off the deep end.

NOTES

THE 16th DAY

As I write this, I have just returned from my rapid early morning walk with my neighbor. "Daily exercise" is a phrase I cringe at, but right now my arms and legs tingle, my head is clear, my outlook is positive — and *joy of living* is a palpable truth. So I give myself the energy of good words: *to exercise is to celebrate life!*

I give myself the daily gift of a two-mile walk on a country road: browsing deer and babbling brook, old barns and open fields. But I can just as easily celebrate life in my own home on an exercise bike, on bustling city streets, or in a commercial gym. It's my attitude that matters. Always it's my attitude.

I will be honest. I don't do that walk every single day. You see, I'm not so much trying to convince *you* of this philosophy as myself. I have great resistance to physical effort. (I began walking at age fifty; that is, only last year.) My commitment wavers and I need my neighbor, who seems to pull me along by the very force of her will. Because I'm competitive, I manage to keep up with her.

I notice the little voices in my head as I walk. The negative ones are frustrating: "My legs hurt; this is too buggy; we ought to slow down; my back itches with sweat." The less noisy, positive voices please me and are beginning to win out: "What a glorious breeze; my legs are moving so smoothly; my breathing is regular; I feel so *good*!"

It occurs to me once again that this is the only life and body I will ever have. I am giving them my love.

WHAT ARE MY IDEAS ABOUT POSITIVE PEOPLE, FEAR, COURAGE, OTHERS' OPINIONS OF ME, AND GOING WITH THE FLOW OF MY LIFE?

H.P. Plans Ahead

The 17th Day

People who believe as I do in the purposefulness of the universe and of each individual life, often remark that "There are no coincidences" or "It was meant to be." They're acknowledging that something divine and inspired happens at every moment of our lives, and each moment we're invited to take part. I say "invited," because through my own arrogance I can refuse the invitation any time I choose. At one time I *always* refused!

As I've become more in tune with this concept, I smile over the lengths to which my Higher Power seems to go for my benefit. (I call Him H.P., because He's become less intimidating and more personal than the God of my childhood.) For example, the co-author of two of my books came into my life just a few months before my husband died. She'd been a professional editor for a long while, and I would be needing those abilities. Now she's editing this book, and says she's doing her best to remove* the arrogance. Also, my book distributor is an old friend. We'd established a surprisingly honest personal relationship over several years — just the kind one would want in a partnership — and there he was, unknowingly preparing for me, setting up his business just when I needed him. And again: I'm so resistant to exercise that I'd never get around to my morning walk if I didn't have a partner. She's been passing my house for years, seemingly just waiting for me to greet her from my front porch and offer to join her.

I have an unfailing belief that *H.P. plans ahead*, that He

---

*Ed. note: Change "remove" to "tone down." I don't want to remove *all* of it!

sets people, places and things in my path for the enhancement of my life *if I'm willing to accept them.* They seem to converge on a point directly in front of me. I know that when I'm willing to pay attention, a new convergence has already formed, ready to lead me on an unexpected path. It makes me wake in the morning with a question: "What do You have for me today?"

Do you remember the connect-the-dots game we played as children, where we followed the numbers until a picture formed that could never have been deduced from the dots alone? My life's like that. When I follow the dots willingly, my life is open to miracles. It is almost effortless. When I decide to veer off on dots of my own design, it becomes difficult to follow through. Roadblocks immediately spring up in my path. I explain the struggle this way: the line *I* want to draw doesn't belong in the picture of my life. And I'm beginning to see a picture forming. I now know that even the sad, horrible, tragic parts of my life are necessary. I'm not able to acknowledge this in the midst of tragedy, but looking back, I begin to believe it must be so.

After I Fail, Then What?

THE 18th DAY

Failure has gotten a bad name. It's often looked upon as some permanent disfigurement, like leprosy or the Scarlet Letter. Remember how an "F" looked on a test? Always written bigger and bolder than other grades, it seemed to pulsate on the paper as if it were alive! "To fail" meant that *I* was a failure, not simply that I'd failed at a particular task. It also implied that I could attain perfection if only I were hard-working and diligent enough.

Thank heaven life isn't so unforgiving as school. Now I can set aside those old beliefs about failure. I can look at it for what it truly is: the completion or incompletion of a task in a way that's unacceptable to my standards. Whenever I fail, I reinforce my (newly discovered) knowledge that I'm not perfect and will never attain perfection. Yes, that knowledge is *new*! I also take the sting out of the experience by making these promises to myself:

1. I will admit my failure.
2. I will evaluate the failure objectively and determine which of my characteristics were involved in causing it.
3. I will determine what I can do differently the next time in similar circumstances.
4. I will not rehash the failure in my mind or put myself down because of it.
5. I will proceed cheerfully with my life.

Number five is the most important, because I must deal with the here and now; the failure is already past history. After I fail, then what? I mean *immediately* after? I used to have a hot bath and a hot toddy, but somewhere along the way that method failed me. Now I usually have a hot bath and a nap, if possible. I wake refreshed, talk over the above points with a friend, and get busy on some favorite project.

Now I'm no longer a complete failure in my own mind; I just have an awful lot of life experiences to learn from!

NOTES

DON'T SUPPORT YOUR SHORTCOMINGS

THE 19th DAY

I've always been a klutz.
I can't make smalltalk.
I have a quick temper.

Have you said something like that repeatedly to yourself? Imagine what power those limitations have over you. I used to believe I was being open and honest when I told you about my shortcomings. I'd go into some detail, explaining that these are the "facts." There's no fighting the facts, I thought. It didn't occur to me that I was giving my limitations power, prestige and permanence!

During my morning walk, my breathing becomes painful and labored as I begin the long trek up the hill to the golf course. I make a joke of it to myself: "I just can't handle Heartbreak Hill!" When I mentioned to a friend that my stamina wasn't improving, she laughed at me (I hate that!). How could I expect to get any better, she wanted to know, if I'm forever focused on the debilitating nature of Heartbreak Hill?

The next morning I approached Heartbreak Hill — I mean that lovely, shaded incline that leads to the golf course. "This is a comfortable, slow rise," I told myself. "My breathing is steady," I reminded me. "I can lengthen my stride a bit," I continued. My body's response was perceptibly different. When "Heartbreak Hill" flickered across my mind, the legs immediately became heavy and unresponsive.

Punkin, my adolescent tomcat, is back up the tree. The last time, he was there four days, becoming progressively more lethargic. Once again he's drooping from the branch, legs dangling on either side of the fork. It's a fifteen-foot drop; his cry is pitiful and weak as he paws half-heartedly at the bark. ''Mama, I can't get down,'' he's meowing. I've explained to him clearly that he's arguing for his limitations and they've gained control of him. Last time, on the fourth day, I brought out a bag of food and shook it. There was an eruption! Out of the fork like a slingshot and down the trunk in a headlong scramble. Punkin had changed his thinking from ''Can't'' to ''Dinner!'', which I imagined him yelling like ''Geronimo!''

Miss Priss, dainty all-white feminine kitty, is crying to him from the doorway. The power of positive thinking, Punkin. When you stop giving your limitations legitimacy, they'll no longer be yours! Am I about to discover if sex can overcome fear?*

NOTES

** Yup! It can!*

Once You've Been A Pickle...

The 20th Day

Recovering alcoholics usually have a way of saying something profound with a memorable twist of humor, such as: "Once you've been a pickle, you can never be a cucumber again!" I like it. Picture the poor pickle bathing itself in numberless pails of water, week after week, becoming less and less briny — only to end up as a lousy, lifeless, depressed, unperky pickle! And the same thing would happen to me. *I must accept myself as I truly am right now.* My past is past; what's done is done; I cannot undo it and I can never go back.

And yet, the fact that I've become a pickle is no reason for not taking responsible action. Helen Keller said: "Life is either a daring adventure, or nothing." Can I ever forget that she was deaf, dumb and blind? *Nothing I have either acquired or lost is a reason for not taking action.* If I tell you the true story of a fine artist who became paralyzed and now paints with the brush between his teeth, do you begin to get my meaning?

Self-acceptance is emphatically *not* a negative, here-I-am-with-all-these-tragedies-that-keep-me-from-fulfilling-my-life-and-ain't-it-awful attitude. It's a positive, life-giving attitude that cries out "I'm going for it!" rather than "I can't because . . ." There are absolutely no reasons for limiting my positive approach to life, only excuses. Once I begin to accept my pickleness — whatever I am right now — then my hindrances and limitations* fade. They become unimportant. No, they become *irrelevant*. The inner turmoil and

---

*Ed. note: alcoholism starts out as a liability, but can end up as an *enormous* asset!

self-pity and blame disappear. Since each limitation and asset must be accepted as it comes, self-acceptance is a lifetime trip, not a single decision.

It bears repeating: I *choose* my attitude. Self-acceptance is a life-embracing, self-loving, self-responsible attitude. If I continue to use my limitations and defects to explain my inaction, they become expensive. They will cost me my life!

So what's a pickle to do?
Become the best damn pickle in the world,
That's who!

NOTES

Quit "Shoulding" On Yourself

THE 21st DAY

"Should," "must," and "ought" are three words that set off red flares of warning in my head. I stiffen immediately when I hear them. They sound as if they're coming from someone else's value system, not mine — and they sound powerfully judgmental. Are they echoes of my parents, or Suburban America, or the package of rules I've attempted to jam myself into? Perhaps they come from the perfect image I want to present to the public. All I know is, the real ME isn't in agreement with those "shoulds"!

When I hear these emotionally loaded words, I pause long enough to phrase the sentence more completely and honestly to myself: "I *should* do that because *they* . . ." You see? There's the problem already. "They" are judging and directing my actions again. Every time I "should" on myself (it really *is* emotional dumping!) and then decline to take the action I've ordered myself to take, I feel guilty. I berate myself for not being the way I'm "supposed" to be and I'm off into my image again instead of simply being me and following my own conscience. The thing is, my head's full of all sorts of rules and roles and recommendations; it's damned hard to know where "I" am in this mess!

When I "should," "must" or "ought," the immediate or at least implied next thought in my head is, "but I don't *want* to!" So I need to check my motives. Are they simple rebellion? Little-girl selfishness? Am I just trying to avoid responsibility or emotional pain? Or would it be *wise* for me to avoid the "should"? I've learned that motives are almost never pure, but I can sometimes sort them out with a bit of honest self-analysis. This is very hard for me to do, because my image of what my motives *ought* to be may have little relationship to the truth. I can be just plain petty. If I decide to call upon an honest friend for feedback, I simply say: "I'm not sure of my motives here. Will you check me out?" (I don't do that very often, because I usually don't like what I hear!)

It helps to rephrase the sentence instead of "shoulding." I say to myself, "I will (or won't) do this because . . ." This starts me thinking of my own values and desires rather than the standards of "those people." Perhaps I'll end up doing exactly what I "should" because it's also what I believe is best — not just because it's been dictated to me. I can avoid resentment and guilt if I know my decision really stems from enlightened self-interest.

I don't like shoulding on myself, so I avoid doing it to others, especially my grown children. When I've heard myself saying "You should . . ." I've even stopped myself in mid-sentence and apologized! If I actually have a helpful alternative for them to think about, aren't they more likely to pay attention if I say, "Here's an alternative to think about"? Doesn't that sound better? It should! (Groan.)

HOW DO I CARE FOR MYSELF? HOW DOES H.P. CARE FOR ME?

The Difference Between "Think" And "Feel"

The 22nd Day

With so many people in therapy and treatment for addiction, the expression of feelings has become a priority. Everyone is "into it"! But there is much confusion. Thoughts and opinions are being interpreted as feelings, and communication is bogging down.

What *are* feelings? Just that. Bodily changes you can feel or sense inside of you. They're usually located from the mouth down; thoughts are located in the head. Feelings are experiences like a dry mouth, thumping heart, twist in the gut, shaky legs. What we *call* a feeling is always our interpretation of our response to a thought or perception. For example, you and I approach a tiny airplane together for our first flight. I think I'm looking forward to the ride; you think we would've been given wings if we were meant to fly. We are both feeling similar sensations: hearts beating rapidly, eyes wide, stomachs fluttery. However, I'm feeling excited, while you're feeling apprehensive. Feelings are value judgments.

To learn the difference between expressing a thought and a feeling, remember that a feeling is usually a single word. *Mad, sad, glad* and *scared* are the basics, but we've evolved hundreds of subtleties for each feeling. *Mad* can be angry, pissed, enraged, irked, frustrated, furious — and so on. Since feelings express the inner you, the words "I feel" can be replaced with the phrase "I am." "I think" can be replaced with "I believe."

For example, "I feel that you are hurting me" is not a feeling, but a thought *about* a feeling. It can be restated this way: "I *believe* that you are hurting me." But you cannot say "I *am* that you are hurting me." To express the feeling itself, you say: "I *feel* hurt" or "I *am* hurt."

We have been taught that feelings are real. We are told we must "own" them, and that other people are negating us in some way when they say to us, "Don't feel that way." All this is true, but more often than not, we pawn off our opinions and beliefs as feelings. "I feel that the new highway will be damaging to my property," for example, gets a Don't-feel-that-way response, and you're off on He-negated-my-feelings rather than recognizing that you were expressing an opinion, not a feeling, in the first place!

This confusion helps to undermine relationships, often sabotoging communication at the outset. "I expressed my feelings and he just got furious" is an all-too-common statement. What was actually *said* to him was, "I feel that *you* are always . . ." (fill in the blanks!) Accusatory opinions masquerading as feelings won't get you very far.

To open up lines of communication, change to "I am" and "I believe" statements, being careful to leave "you" out of the sentence entirely — unless you're giving an outright compliment. This will be more difficult than you expect. But if you listen carefully to yourself and your friend as you talk, you'll begin to hear the difference between a thought and a feeling. With practice, you'll learn to identify, acknowledge and even state your beliefs (opinions) for what they are, rather than mislabeling them as feelings. Once you do, you'll be amazed at how quickly communication improves!

Nurture That Littlest Voice

The 23rd Day

Do you have several voices forever warring in your head? I don't mean auditory hallucinations, but the silent thoughts that argue with one another and do battle over you. Mine control and assassinate my character, my behavior, my personality and thoughts, plans, decision-making abilities and attitudes. Everything. Unkind at the very least, they're often downright nasty.

One is clearly *parental* and used to be the loudest. It begins every sentence with "You should" or "You shouldn't" and is accompanied by instant guilt. It has a partner I think of as my Rebellious Little Girl, whose stock-in-trade is, "I can if I want to" and "You can't make me!"

My father often repeated this miserable little poem to me:

> There was a little girl and she had a little curl
> Right in the middle of her forehead.
> When she was good she was very, very good
> But when she was bad she was horrid.

I know those two inner voices are intimately connected with that ditty. I've talked to a friend who got the same garbage thrown at her, and we agree that its only purpose was to shame us into submission when we were "horrid." What a rotten thing to do to a little girl!

Then there's my Honest Conscience voice. It isn't always loud and doesn't attempt to be persuasive. It states my moral convictions with such comments as, "That would be harmful" or "That's the right thing to do."

Two other voices are Janus-faced twins. One side is my insecurity: "You'll never be able to," "You're not smart enough," "That isn't possible." The other I lovingly call my Cheerleader. It says things like "Bravo!", "You can do it," and "Go for it!" That voice has helped me accomplish several good things in my life.

There's yet another pair of voices ever-present in my head. One I call the Observer — the one that sits back, non-judgmentally listening and watching and recording all these goings on. But the last, littlest voice is the most imporant. It's the one I think of as ME. It gives me certain kinds of messages: I am, I feel, I believe, I will, I want, I can. This is the only voice I care to nurture.

The results of this self-care have been miraculous. Whenever the other voices begin to murmur, I simply call forth ME and begin an "I" thought. Now, after several years of constant awareness and vigilance, only one voice remains steadfastly in my head, and that is ME. The Observer is there too, of course, and sometimes the Cheerleader — but that's it. I've gained some inner peace because I've practiced calling upon that littlest voice. Getting rid of all those warring voices and finding a core that seems to be ME doesn't happen by accident; it *does* happen through conscious, self-caring effort.

Things I Don't Have Time For

The 24th Day

My husband literally "nailed down" this little bit of philosophy for me. We had just built a large addition to our house, and he had no time to finish the siding. It was a three- to four-day job. He couldn't afford to take that much time from his regular construction business, but he wanted the siding completed before many rains fell. Besides, he'd be damned if he'd pay someone else for something he could very well do himself!

So he allotted fifteen minutes a day to siding. Before he even came in from work each evening, I would hear the steady rapping of his hammer. I'd know it was time to put on the vegetables because in a quarter of an hour there he'd be: tired, flushed, obviously pleased with himself — and in less than a month the job was finished to his satisfaction.

I'm not so disciplined! But I make inroads on my laziness by attacking many ongoing chores in fifteen-minute increments — like file-purging, drawer-cleaning, curtain-making, room-painting. Yes, especially room-painting. One wall a day, and the furniture can go back in place immediately. There's less fuss and disruption. Even the pictures can be rehung in an hour.

It's a fine system, and will become even more satisfying when I stop having the little foot-dragging discussions in my head: "Now? Why now? Can't it wait? I'm going to be interrupted if I start now. Yes, it *would* matter. It's too big a project. I've got to do something else first. Who thought up this only-fifteen-minutes crap anyhow?"

And then I break the inertia and get on with it. It keeps both my garbage and my anxiety at manageable levels!

NOTES

Still Out Of Step

The 25th Day

I've always felt different and unique. One Christmas my playmate got fuzzy white fur mittens; my mother gave me a set of classical books. I was so envious! But by noon her mittens were a muddy mess and I'd settled by the fire for an absorbing afternoon with *Tess of the D'Urbervilles*. At my progressive school in the 40's we wore jeans every day; "normal" girls wore frilly dresses or crisp uniforms. But my school had a horse and pony; theirs didn't! I never knew what was the "right" thing to wear, or the "in" music. Everyone else shrieked over Marlon Brando in *On the Waterfront*, but I fell in love with Lee J. Cobb. Because the other kids were astonished by my opinions, I learned to keep them to myself. I became a loner; I didn't fit; I was always uneasy. What went into smalltalk anyway? I hadn't the foggiest idea.

One evening when I was twenty-nine, my brother-in-law and I were talking together at an ultra-fancy formal party. He remarked that he felt awkward and out of place among all these sophisticated people. I was stunned! No one had ever admitted a thing like that to me before. I acknowledged with relief that I felt the same way. Just then we caught sight of our reflections in a full-length mirror across the room. We looked elegant, relaxed, self-confident — and sophisticated. Did this mean that other people's outsides didn't match their insides either? It was a revelation.

Now I know that I don't so much march to a different drummer; I *am* that drummer. Now I hear my own softer beat more often than society's loud thumping to conform. I only need to assure myself that I'm not hurting anyone else because of my individuality. Everyone is his own drummer, and we all probably feel much the same about being unique. I no longer disapprove of others for not doing things the way I would. I accept the differences. In fact, I'm stimulated by them. Even smalltalk has become possible now that I know I don't have to measure up to others' expectations.

I *am* different. I have special skills and wonderful qualities to offer, and I'm well along the rocky road to self-acceptance. (Except there's all the difference in the world between *saying* it's okay to be me and *knowing* at the core of my being that this is so.)

And I *am* the same. I became part of the human race the day I discovered you sometimes felt uneasy, too.

NOTES

What Are You Pretending Not To Know?

The 26th Day

Punkin the orange kitten has acquired a new maturity around the eyes and a definite swagger to his walk. Miss Priss, my pure white lady-kitten, is gentle and demure. Butter wouldn't melt in her mouth! Recently, Punkin has taken to chasing after Miss Priss, biting her on the neck until she yowls. My friend remarked that orange-and-white kittens would be most attractive, but I was vehement: "They're much too young!" My friend snidely observed that Punkin appeared to be the final authority on the subject. Flash of insight! Denial shattered, I phoned the vet to arrange for an operation or two.

A silly example? Perhaps. But denial seems to be just as absurd in more severe and even life-threatening circumstances.

> A bride goes starry-eyed into a marriage, though everyone else knows the groom's an irresponsible bum.
>
> A wife denies her husband's alcoholism, though he's never sober after five-thirty.
>
> A man pooh-poohs physical changes, though the symptoms of severe disease are classic and obvious.

Denial isn't simply *saying* something is not so, it's *being certain* that it's not so! That's how capable the mind is of deceiving itself. Even the most skillful confrontation may not be able to break through to let in the light of reality.

As my friend spoke of Punkin's expertise, the only question I needed to ask myself flashed through my mind: *What am I pretending not to know?* For some reason that question gets through my defenses and denial in a most effective way. It untangles me from the trees so I can observe the forest.

I have often used it to re-evaluate my life when I'm suffering from high stress and discomfort and don't know the reason on any conscious level. It draws out surprisingly clear answers — answers that seem to have escaped me before:

> This person is *not* a friend after all.
> This job has *no* future for me.
> This illness *is* serious.
> This time it *won't* be different.
> This cat *is* pregnant!

NOTES

There Are No Victims, Only Volunteers

The 27th Day

Victimhood is extraordinarily satisfying to the sufferer accepting the role. It's suitably attention-getting and effortless, although some energy is expended in bitching and complaining about "those" circumstances or people. It presumes that *all* responsibility for *any* nefarious deed belongs to "them." If you see yourself as a victim, you automatically absolve yourself of all blame, and place it squarely on the shoulders of the other person or society (which so richly deserves it!).

Does your victimhood spring from the timeworn (outworn!) belief that there's nobility in suffering? Or from a philosophy that things *outside of you* can "make" you do something you don't want to do, or feel something you don't want to feel? Are you convinced, Victim, that you have no choices at all? Ah, helpless innocent!

Victims hunt for cages without bars and then joyously — nay, triumphantly — rush in to lie prostrate. "But what can I *do?*" Victim wails. The answer is simple: just about anything but what you're doing now. At the very least, stand on your head and whistle "Dixie"; it confuses the opposition.

"But where can I *go?*" Victim continues. Again the answer is simple: there are seven gorgeous continents to choose from. "But I can't *afford* it!" Victim tries again. Sure you can, but you don't want the inconvenience, discomfort, embarrassment or responsibility!

I remember counseling a young man who had lost his hands in an industrial accident. He had prostheses, and was skilled at using them, but he couldn't go out to find work because his wife wouldn't buckle his pants belt for him. Her lack of caring was a cruel tragedy, he believed, and I was called upon to sympathize with his ongoing helplessness, and get her to behave. He became enraged after we talked. And all I did was suggest he wear suspenders. (But the very next day he did!)

What I'm getting at is that we all have unlimited choices. *We are responsible.* Here's a graphic way to think of it: whenever you point an accusing finger, there are three fingers pointing back at you. I state categorically: *there are no victims*. None. Never! Only volunteers eager to play the role.

When do you stop being able to play Victim convincingly? Now. Since you've read this. How come? Because you're no longer a helpless innocent; you've been told. You can no longer be "done unto" because at every turn, with every breath, you know you are *making choices*: to go, to stay, to say yes or no, to place yourself in a situation or to refuse. Take another look. There's never been a lock on that door.

THE RUBBER DUCK THEORY

THE 28th DAY

A plump, yellow rubber duck sits on the corner of my bathtub, the gift of a young woman who presented it as insurance against my ever drinking again. It's an odd and humorous symbol of my sobriety.

Several recovering alcoholics, all sober for more than five years, were having coffee late one night at the diner. Conversation turned to the way our mothers had treated us. If we delved deeply enough, surely we could each discover some definitive experience that had "caused" our alcoholism? There's a standing joke that "good Christian families" must be the cause, since we'd each come from one. Now we were after something simpler and more measurable.

We decided to share childhood traumas. Mine was the birth of my baby brother. I'd been an only child for five years, so you can imagine how the arrival of this kid struck me. Indeed, I've totally blacked out the first year of his life following one horrid vision: my grandmother laying the thing in my mother's arms as she sits in her bed, newly arrived home from the hospital.

Suddenly I saw my brother splashing joyously in the tub with his rubber ducky. I told my friends how I'd viciously twisted the metal squeaker out of that toy in a fit of jealousy and resentment. That rubber duck galvanized the group; the chemist among us called for an immediate investigation. Scientific study gleaned the following statistics: five remembered a sibling with a rubber ducky; all seven vehemently denied having had one of their very own. The six alcoholics at the next table assured us they had been neglected, too. Even more revealing, a non-alcoholic spouse remembered her own little duck with obvious affection. We agreed that further investigation was unnecessary. The evidence was conclusive: *Being deprived of a rubber duck in childhood causes alcoholism!*

Yes, we liked the Rubber Duck Theory, because it "solved" so many problems all at once.

1. It was measurable; you either had a duck or you didn't.
2. It explained absolutely everything.
3. It absolved each of us of responsibility by placing the blame squarely elsewhere (on Mom!).
4. It would pay many a shrink's rent. Think of the number of (lucrative!) sessions you could spend in recounting your anger toward your mother for not giving you a rubber duck!

The Rubber Duck Theory may seem like a silly joke, but it isn't. We may be using some more sophisticated form of it every day to avoid taking charge of our lives. They're such great excuses: child abuse, incest, poverty, broken home, no education, a physical disability, neglect or abandonment. It seems that we'd like to wait *until our past gets better. Then* we'll act. The little geranium and the rubber duck have a lot in common, don't they?

And that's the moral of this story: *nothing* in my past life has the power to immobilize me now. I'm the only one who can keep me stuck. No matter what I've endured, *all the repairs are up to me.* From this day forward I'm responsible for my own actions; that dumb duck isn't holding onto my feet!

AM I A VICTIM OR AM I SELF-RESPONSIBLE?

What's My Bottom Line?

The 29th Day

My self-esteem used to be nonexistent. With no values of my own, only what I was taught to follow, I simply did what I thought was expected of me. I people-pleased and made believe, building a tough wall of bluff around myself. I had no idea what the person named Judy wanted or needed, what I believed in or where I was going. Not so much a phony as a person without identity, I didn't discover an authentic "me" until I stopped drinking — and could no longer keep hiding from myself.

"Bottom-lining" became a practical method of discovering who I was and what I stood for. I could say to myself, "I won't accept that unacceptable behavior." Then I learned to say it out loud, and finally I was able to follow through with action. I began to like myself, because I was treating myself kindly. The more self-esteem and self-worth I gained, the higher I was able to raise a bottom line. At first I was simply aggressive about my position; later I learned to choose my own actions for myself rather than demanding something of someone else.

Now I know I have a bottom line *in every single circumstance*, whether or not I recognize it. Saying and doing nothing means I'll accept the lowest line someone else decides to hand me. For example, you're going to hear from me publicly if you're in front of me with fifty items in a twelve-item checkout line, but I'll still accept a lousy restaurant dinner in silence. Only if there's frost in the center, or a very large bug, will I send it back (and I still find myself asking if I'm worth the temporary embarrassment).

No one knows better than I that self-esteem and self-worth are gained through hard-fought battles and daily affirmation. I'm still developing my values, so I may not immediately know where I stand. I may have to pause and ask myself, "What's my bottom line?" Sometimes I'd like to compromise my standards just to keep peace, but I'm not able to do that any longer. I don't want to give myself those resentments and low feelings. I'm the only one I have to live with every single day, and I'm worth more than that.

NOTES

We Teach Others How To Treat Us

THE 30th DAY

We are treated exactly as we wish to be. We ask for and even *demand* a certain kind of treatment. We wouldn't have it any other way. In fact, if we wanted it another way, *it would be*! It has everything to do with our "bottom line." We all have one. It says, "This is it; past this point you absolutely may not go with me, no matter what!" And everyone knows instinctively that we mean it. Each of us has a different bottom line — and that's the whole point. *The higher the bottom, the better the treatment!*

A stunningly attractive young friend of mine has been telling me of her boss' not-so-subtle sexual harrassment in the offices of a large corporation. His behavior has been offensive to a number of women. However, when I asked what he'd pulled on her, she merely laughed. "He wouldn't dare. He knows how fast I'd blow the whistle on him!"

Had she told him up front what she'd do? No, he simply knew from her whole demeanor, from her attitude toward herself. She's obviously willing to tackle issues head on — and often does — and she's willing to accept the consequences of her acts even when they're not popular.

We began to contrast her behavior with that of the other women. In very similar ways, they all act like doormats. "Walk on me once more, I'll scrunch down a little further" is the prevailing attitude.

What do they say? *Nothing!* They explain that they're ignoring him, but their silence has simply let him know that what he's doing is okay. Silence is usually viewed as consent, not disapproval.

What about body language? *Defenseless!* With heads lowered and shoulders hunched, they may consider themselves demure and ladylike, but they're actually announcing clearly, "I won't stick up for my rights!"

What do their eyes signal? *Submission!* In his presence they usually stare at the floor or his belt buckle.

What do they do? Again, *nothing!* Certainly no protest to his supervisor. When he's abusive, they don't even remove themselves from his presence, which would be entirely appropriate.

Sometimes they protest feebly to each other, bitching and complaining in corners, but they're living a lie (threats or protests are always lies if not followed by action), and they lack credibility even with each other. They believe that this job — complete with sexual harrassment — is more valuable than their self-worth and integrity.

These women also believe that they are *blameless*, as well as helpless to change their circumstances. If this were so, then my friend would be in identical circumstances — but she isn't. Her boss is a respectful gentleman with her, because she allows no less.

So how can these other doormats roll themselves into upright mats with some stiffness of purpose? By determining that "it" will never happen again without appropriate consequences, which may at first mean a simple comment followed by an action. If a battered woman goes to court *the very first time*, then her man immediately faces the consequences of his vicious, unacceptable act. The second time must be the last. If the woman *knows* she will follow through publicly, then a second time is much less likely to occur.

A bottom line, no matter how faint, is present in every single circumstance of my life. If my action follows swiftly, the other person gets the message and my own self-esteem increases. It gets progressively easier to act, until I seem to gain an aura of self-determination like the one my attractive friend has. She's a gentle young woman. You only catch the glint of steel in her eyes once you've pushed her too far.

Time For Self-Pity

The 31st Day

Self-pity is a self-serving, immobilizing and fraudulent emotion. Why fraudulent? Because it must be nurtured and fussed over and warmed up in order to maintain its intensity. We're all aware of that when we watch someone else indulging in it, but it takes on a more positive character when it's our own. It has real power; it feels so *good!* It's a comforting, warm blanket that we wrap around and hug to ourselves — *since no one else can possibly understand!*

I've been an expert on self-pity. For almost fifteen years it was what I did best. I nurtured a litany of miseries to sob myself to sleep. Crazy though it may seem now, back then it gave me a reason for living, focusing heaps of emotional attention on me — and how I craved attention!

"Well, then, I just won't feel sorry for myself any more" doesn't seem to work. A fine decision on paper, it ignores the perverted pleasure self-pity provides. It *is* difficult to get rid of, but there is a way. *Give in to it!* This method worked so well for me that I'm (almost) unable to indulge myself in this stupid pastime any more!

Giving in to self-pity is best done all by yourself, in your bed with the covers pulled up tightly over your head. Now allow yourself fifteen* minutes to wallow — *by the clock*. At the end of that period, jump up, wash your face, swing your arms, take a few deep breaths and get out of the house *fast*! If you do this every single day without fail, you'll soon discover that fifteen minutes is a *very* long time to slosh around in the same old smelly garbage. Finally you'll

*Not twenty, not even sixteen!

become bored with it. Honestly. You'll stop feeling sorry for yourself and get on with your life. That's just the way it works.

NOTES

Living Rent-Free In My Lagoon

The 32nd Day

I have held onto—no, welcomed and embraced—resentments so all-encompassing that I didn't even know I had them. They *became* me! I wasn't filled with ordinary anger; I repeatedly dragged rumbling rages up from the depths of my being. Otherwise the original anger would have long since faded away.

To resent comes from a Latin word meaning "to feel again." It's the other side of that petty coin of self-pity. Resentment makes me feel important and alive, once again the center of the universe. I focus righteous rage on "those people": How could she? How dare he? Look what they did to me! I dump responsibility on someone else and there I am, halo in place, helpless, blameless and done unto. (Uh-oh. Sounds like Victim rearing its ugly head again!)

Where's the harm? Resentments are negative and damaging to *me*, and I'm no longer willing to fill my head with warmed-over, rehashed and recooked garbage. That's what resentments are: *garbage!* To me, the old phrase "harboring resentments" conjures up this picture: the arms of a welcoming bay protecting barges full of rancid old junk. When I drag up old resentments, it's said that the offending person is "living rent-free in my head." So are those barges residing rent-free. Does it make sense to let them pollute the peaceful lagoon of my mind?

It's time to drag those barges out to sea and dump the garbage for good. Time to get rid of the *habit* of resentment, because that's what it is: a very nasty habit! The first thing I must do is become honest with myself: am I *willing* to give up those self-important resentments? Am I willing to let go of my righteousness and innocence? If so, then I can call upon several time-honored tugboats (if this metaphor isn't becoming too putrid!):

One: I can head off the resentment. This means that I express my hurt or anger to the offending person *when the incident happens*, instead of smuggling it home to examine and mull over at my leisure. Facing the person immediately means I'm dealing with the issue. Once dealt with, it dissipates and becomes past history.

Two: I can review the incident — once! — and then set it aside, concentrating instead on more positive and constructive thoughts.

Three: If I can't confront the person immediately, I talk the whole thing over with a friend, making sure I *listen to myself* as I describe the incident. It always sounds so different when it's out of my obsessive head. If the situation still needs confronting, my friend may have some objective and practical suggestions. (I don't choose people as friends who'll hand me, "You poor thing, how terrible!")

Four: If a resentment insists on resurfacing regardless (never forgetting that it doesn't just happen accidentally; my will brings it forth again) then I can pray for that person. It's hard for me to do, but I'm learning that it's impossible for a positive prayer and a negative emotion to occupy my head at the very same time.

Five: If the resentment hasn't been permanently "deep-sixed" by these methods, then I spend several minutes in soul-searching with paper and pencil. I concentrate on the part *I* played in the drama. Did I place myself in a foolish position? Trust a dishonest businessman? Give someone the undeserved status of friend? What about my own motives? What am I pretending not to know about my own participation? I write it all down. It's rough!

No one lives rent-free in my mind for any length of time. Not any more. Those barges of garbage get tugged over the horizon. Regurgitated feelings don't deserve more than fifteen minutes of my attention. If I call upon those five tugboats whenever I need them, the lagoon of my mind will remain clean and clear.

Start Your Day Anytime

THE 33rd DAY

Maintaining my mind within a twenty-four-hour period is marvelous for planning and productivity; keeping my mind in the moment is even more wonderful for the pure enjoyment of living. But once in a while I come up against a day that's so rotten, miserable and pointless that it doesn't deserve the courtesy of my attention. Nothing's going right. I can't even turn around without knocking something over. Talk about crying over spilt milk? That was a quart of honey that just broke. Try cleaning up *that* stuff when you're late for an appointment and your darling little kittens have begun to tiptoe through it! Maybe I'm wallowing in self-pity, steeped in resentment, coming down with the flu or just plain miserable. Whatever the circumstances, you get the idea: I should've stayed in bed!

If I'm truly committed to living one day at a time, then I have a solution. It's a game that works, because it puts my life back into perspective: *I start my day right now, after the misery*! I realize it's merely mental gymnastics, but it still helps me to eject the rotten things from my mind, placing them firmly behind me in "yesterday." Why not a battle cry? "Agony behind; anticipation before!" When I turn my back on the garbage, I can face the immediate future more cheerfully. Right away I'm in a more positive frame of mind. So what if it's five o'clock in the afternoon? Dusk is a down period for me anyway. I'll make five the midnight of that miserable day — and this very moment the sunrise of a new one!

NOTES

I Don't Tempt Fate

The 34th Day

I think I understand something about probabilities. If I flip a coin, it has a fifty-fifty chance of coming up "heads" each time it's flipped. If I toss it a hundred times, it can *conceivably* come up one hundred heads or one hundred tails, but because of the "laws of chance," the probability of its actually happening is practically nil. (I wouldn't want to spend a lifetime trying to make it happen just once!)

Not long ago I rushed to my car, already late, disorganized and harried, vaguely wondering if I'd forgotten anything because I would be gone all day. By the time I'd driven a couple of miles, my head was in full debate:

"You left the coffee pot on."
"I don't do that any more."
"This time you did."
"It'll be okay; nothing will happen; it's been left on lots of times before."
"This time it may be different."
"I'm late already."
"Is it your intention to gamble with the safety of your beloved house?"
"WHAT?"

I slammed on the brakes and drove back. Sure enough, I'd left the coffee pot on.

How often in the past have I had similar internal debates, filling myself with vague unease, relieved when nothing happened? I hate that feeling, and I'm no longer willing to put myself through the anxiety. I no longer intend consciously to tempt fate.

My husband expressed it succinctly. He'd taken to buckling

his seat belt on even the shortest trips, long before the New Jersey seat belt law had been passed. I asked him how come the change in attitude from his usual cavalier defiance? He said it just struck him one day. He didn't want to find himself hurtling toward the windshield, his very last thought being "You damned fool!"

NOTES

THE 35th DAY

"Sought through prayer *and meditation* to improve our conscious contact with God as we understood Him, praying only for knowledge of His will for us and the power to carry that out." (italics mine)

I quote Step Eleven of the Twelve Suggested Steps of the Anonymous programs because I tell myself I live these steps, but do I? Only the parts I want to, it would seem, because I've been resisting this meditation business all my life. It has something to do with its being "foreign," I think — an Eastern approach to life that's uncomfortable for me. It has something to do with fear of the unknown, and not wanting to be out of control, and maybe there's some plain old defiance. Whatever my resistance, I've avoided meditation, and it's been my loss.

Just this year I've begun to meditate. It takes discipline, because I'm not used to the concept and make the excuse that "I can't find the time." (I've begun to ignore that nonsense.) My practice is very basic: I sit erect in the center of my peaceful stone house — body relaxed, hands resting palms upward in my lap. Sometimes I hold a meditation stone. I follow an undirected meditation, that is without a word (mantra) that I repeat. Eyes not quite closed, I focus on the rug in front of me and on my breathing, while I allow thoughts to drift by. This is not easy! I discover that my head is aswarm with ideas: thoughts, thoughts about thinking, comments to myself about my squinting eyelids. I notice a car going by, the drip of a faucet. Quick as a flash I think about traffic or calling a plumber! Then I think about *thinking* about the traffic, et cetera. What mental convolutions! And I again concentrate on my breathing. Twenty minutes goes by easily and the time seems ''right'' because I haven't checked my watch. When meditation is over, it's simply over.

It's very evident that I haven't let go. It is a process, and my ego is at the center of the struggle. Many, many knowledgeable people have written books about meditation, and there are many experienced guides to help me if I ask. And I will, someday. Asking is important to my growth, but I won't ask yet. Not yet!

In a short time, several wonderful changes have taken place. Focusing on the ''now'' has become immeasurably easier. I have more mental and physical energy and, paradoxically, I've become more peaceful. I sense more contact with my Higher Power, but I still intellectualize the whole process. How can I have more contact if I'm not taking an active role? Can't I just accept? Apparently not! So once again I learn something about myself that I already knew. My meditation time is valuable. I know that now.

WHAT'S MY BOTTOM LINE? AM I FILLED WITH SELF-PITY AND RESENTMENT? HAVE I BEGUN TO MEDITATE?

PUT IT ON PAPER

THE 36th DAY

I can never attain true clarity of mind or serenity of soul, but at least I can strive for them. One of the methods I use is writing. It's a curious thing: once I take a thought out of my head and commit it to paper, my mind immediately calms down. Sometimes the problem even disappears for good. Reading over my notes later, I'm astonished. Is that what I'd been thinking? Problems have less power over me when they hit the reality of black on white. Once I've written down the day's circumstances, I'm left with a less cluttered mind. It's very satisfying.

I use two methods of writing to reduce anxiety. One is a daily activities list, which I update each morning with my second cup of coffee. This list is task-oriented, the duties of the day in organized form. Anything left undone is moved to tomorrow. Procrastination becomes very obvious when the same thing is moved forward every single day. It becomes priority Number One. Now I carry a handsome leather planning and appointments diary. It keeps my schedule. It has plain paper for ideas that would be lost if they weren't recorded immediately. With this notebook, my anxiety is reduced to practically nothing. Heaven help me if I ever lose it!

The other method I use regularly is a bedtime notebook. I know many people keep a free-association journal, but mine is a kind of shorthand version. Each night I meditate on the personal aspects of my day, writing only my conclusions on the pad: what I felt, what amends I need to make. Sometimes it's an abbreviated personal inventory too, headed by a single word like "pride" or "hurt" or "ego," to remind me of the negative characteristic that fouled the day and needs work.

This writing takes regular practice; it didn't come easily. Putting down feelings, attitudes and priorities was a chore until I discovered how much better I always feel afterwards. I become both more peaceful and more energetic, because I don't have to keep reminding myself of my responsibilities. I think of my brain as a computer with just so many bytes. If all the grey cells are filled with the daily stuff, how can I be open to new opportunities? They won't even *register*! So I follow these two simple writing routines for my emotional comfort and to add to the joy of living. They don't take long, and the results are well worth it.

NOTES

I Changed My Mind

The 37th Day

I was taught a number of very serious things when I was young, some of which have stuck with me despite all subsequent evidence to the contrary:

*If I step on a crack, I'll break my mother's back. (You may still catch me assiduously avoiding every one, hesitating and then taking big half-jumps.)

*On Christmas Eve I become anxious if the weather is bad, because of the difficulties the reindeer may have.

*A little bone sticks up in my stomach to catch all my chewing gum if I swallow it. Really! Did I ever study the intestinal tract during freshman year biology!

And I learned *never to go back on my word*. I don't remember the how or why of it, but this was hammered home to me. "Make up your mind and stick with it" was the message. Presumably I was being taught responsibility and decision-making but, as usual, I interpreted this to be an absolute, all-or-nothing principle. It has since caused me real problems both with my children and with other adults. Undoing childhood dogmas is so damned difficult!

For example, when I overreacted to my children's behavior, hastily warning them of dire consequences, I painted myself into a corner and ended up making believe I'd never said anything. Talk about inconsistency! How much better if I had remarked, "I've changed my mind; that was too strict. Instead, I'd like you to . . ." And so, too, with business associates. It's taken me several decades to learn to say, "After further reflection, now that I have more facts to go on . . ." What's the big deal, anyway? My need to be right at all costs, I suspect. And the cost is too high!

Admitting I've changed my mind is a step toward getting rid of my protective self-image — my mask of maturity, perfection and invulnerability. I see *your* flaws and imperfections and know they're okay; they make you unique. Why can't I accept mine? If you really knew me, would you like me? Good heavens, if I admitted to the real me, what would *I* think?

It's a hard-fought step toward accepting my own humanity, but when I leave my self-imposed pedestal I become closer to other people. They can reach out to me rather than straining to reach up. (And I thought this essay was just going to be about changing my mind!)

NOTES

I Was Wrong

THE 38th DAY

When I was small, my father and I played many educational games. If I didn't know the answer to something, we made an exciting project out of looking it up in the dictionary, encyclopedia or almanac. It was great fun; I still get a kick out of research. Early on, I also got the idea that I could, in fact *must*, get it right. If I were paying attention, being responsible, doing my job — I'd get it *right!*

I never discussed this with anyone. It seemed to me the message was too clear: Only stupid people got it wrong. I usually received A's in school, and the few times I took home a B it was obviously a sign that I was doing it wrong. That didn't sit well with my parents. It's no wonder that I became very black-and-white in my thinking, and saved face by never, ever admitting to a mistake.

I was thirty-five when I read Step Ten of the Twelve Suggested Steps of the Anonymous programs: "Continued to take personal inventory and *when we were wrong promptly admitted it.*" [Italics mine.] These were steps for everyone. If they mentioned the possibility of being wrong, at least one other person must be having my problem. This was actually a surprise to me; I had considered myself unique. I was too private a person to talk out loud about wrongs and mistakes.

How I gagged on "I was wrong!" But what an immediate relief it was, no longer having to put up a false front! I don't have to strive for perfection any more; I'm free to be merely human, doing my conscientious best. Another step in getting rid of my ego, my self-protective image. Thirty-five years before I learned this simple truth!

I've also noticed that other people rush to my defense

with excuses when I admit to being wrong: "Well, you're new at this; you couldn't have known." As I become more vulnerable and admit to my imperfections, I become more acceptable. I don't need the protection I spent so many years building, layer upon layer. Life if full of delightful, comforting surprises. I believe I really *do* learn something new every day!

NOTES

NEVER ASK WHY

THE 39th DAY

There seem to be three kinds of "why" questions, and not one of them performs the function that I keep hoping it will. One is the "Why is the world like this?" kind of question that attempts to get at the Creator's motives. How can a mere human comprehend His motivation? Such questions make fine intellectual games, but serve no other real purpose.

The second kind is the accusatory "Why did you do that?" It's an equally purposeless question that merely triggers defensiveness and rationalization. It's great for venting frustration and especially good for starting an argument, but is that the only way I can relate to that person? If it is, I might need to reconsider that particular relationship.

The third kind of "why" is the most intriguing. Thousands of books have been written and millions of hours of therapy expended on "Why do I do this?" (Drink too much, become violent, gamble, play the victim, set myself up for failure, *et cetera*.) This is a marvelous game! It can be played by one or many, for fun or profit. The implication is clear: *If I knew, then I could do.* Have you ever heard an alcoholic's family (or his shrink!) say, "When we find out *why* he drinks, he'll be able to stop?" That's patently absurd. In order to stop, one simply doesn't pick up the first drink, one day at a time. The "whys" are irrelevant. In fact, if energy is focused on them, productive change can be avoided for years or forever!

My rule goes like this: *Never* ask why, not of God, myself or another human being. It will only send me off on a wild goose chase. (Since I've acquired a gaggle of *tame* geese, I know how pointless that must be.) The practical alternative to asking the three irrelevant whys is to ask "what" questions instead. "What" implies action:

> Not, why did God do this, but *what* shall I do about it? Accept? Grieve? Rejoice?
>
> Not, why did you do that, but *what benefit* did you get from the behavior?
>
> Not, why am I this way, but *what* can I do to change it today?

"Why" leaves me impotent; "what" gives me room to act.

NOTES

ROTTEN THINGS

THE 40th DAY

The comfortable management of my life is of constant interest to me. I don't like being anxious. I don't like feeling guilty. I don't like doing what I don't like to do! Nevertheless, lousy things in my life need to be accomplished, and putting them off simply adds to my anxiety and guilt.

These crummy things come in all sizes and shapes: purging business files, attending a funeral, confronting a friend. The list is endless, because I have strong negative reactions to a lot of nit-picky things. I don't imply that this is a good trait; I simply acknowledge that it is true of me.

Being solution-minded, I have come up with a brilliant answer to the problem of handling miserable jobs. (Daily-living stuff like washing dishes and picking up your room cannot be put in the same category; it's best treated mindlessly and ritualistically.) The specially awful things I treat as priorities, limiting myself to doing *just one rotten thing every day!*

This plan of attack has several advantages: first, I reduce my anxiety and guilt. Second, I get the damned thing done! Third, I save the rest of each day for good stuff. Last — and best — I accomplish three hundred and sixty-five rotten things every year. That's a number to be reckoned with!

NOTES

ABDICATE!

THE 41st DAY

Maybe I was just tired of doing what others expected of me, fielding several roles and feeling guilty whenever I couldn't pull it off (which was most of the time, because at least one of us was expecting me to be perfect!).

One day I decided to abdicate. (With abdication, there's absolutely no going back. Just ask an ex-king!) I put a note on the kitchen table that went something like this: "I quit! I am no longer a housewife and a mother." It must've said a few more things, because I was pretty disgusted. I had a full-time job, and was going to night school as well as having a house, husband and three teenagers to care for — and somehow nothing had changed, except a few new responsiblities had been added.

When my husband came home, he read my note and immediately offered to help with dinner. That was fine, I said, because otherwise I'd be preparing for me alone; if he made salad, I'd do meat for two. That suited him fine. When my daughter arrived, she set the table — and I started hamburgers for three.

One son glanced at the manifesto and got a bit panicky, wanting to know if that meant laundry, too. I didn't bother to answer, and pretty soon he was off to the washer, trailing bluejeans behind him. He cut up vegetables and I put on another hamburger. My other son didn't eat with us for a couple of days. I think he expected me to worry about his diet, but I didn't. I had truly abdicated. No guilt. No worry. The kingdom could function without me.

It's a shame I let things get that far out of hand. I now realize I could have relinquished this role by degrees and allowed everyone the experience of taking on one small responsibility at a time. I don't know why I didn't know that. In any case, I don't reign over much but my own self these days. Sometimes "family" gets mad because I no longer take on other people's responsibilities, but I've truly given up being Supermom, because it's just a colossal ego trip. What a relief!

NOTES

THE FORTUNE COOKIE PRINCIPLE

THE 42nd DAY

I can put off just about anything — for *months*. But a niggling little anxiety begins to blossom at the base of my brain. At its crescendo, I have dreams about not graduating (now thirty years behind me) because I haven't finished the last term paper. My mind begins to feel like wet cotton batting as I continue to procrastinate. I berate myself. I obsess. I ask why, WHY am I doing this to me? Why can't I just settle myself down to this miserable task? I forget my own rule: *Never ask why*. Instead I repeat my litany of justifications and add a couple of new ones. Once again I run to an auction, to the phone, to a book or a meeting or a movie or to bed. Anyplace where, for a little while longer, I can just pull the mental blanket over my head and avoid my responsibility. When the anguish gets too great, I'll get to it. But must I always wait for pain? Just for once, can't I act out of common sense?

Some very important tax papers had been preying on my mind. (That phrase is a perfect description; they were preying just as a vulture does, tearing little strips of flesh and brain bit by bit.) Thinking the papers were already overdue, I'd spent a good deal of energy manufacturing excuses, composing brilliant letters of explanation in my head. I'd become increasingly anxious and was beginning to ask "why" questions, a sure sign that I was once again in deep trouble.

A close friend and I went out for Chinese food. I believe implicitly in fortune cookie messages (unless perchance they don't live up to my expectations). I even like their taste! Do you know the rule for fortune cookies? You must choose the one placed closest to you by the waiter; taking one from the far side of the plate gives an inaccurate fortune. I cracked open my cookie with my usual excitement and slid out this little comment:

YOU WILL FIND A SOLUTION
TO A DIFFICULT PROBLEM.

Great! I need it *now*! What could be the solution to those tax papers? They were certainly my most pressing problem.

Arriving home, I pulled the file. I hadn't inspected the offending papers for several months, and made an amazing discovery. I had four more days to go until the filing deadline! I slept blissfully that night.

When dawn came, I was energized. I committed myself absolutely to this one "rotten thing" for the day. The information fell into place as easily as . . . Well, it was just easy. Three quarters of an hour of honest concentration and all was completed, typed, copied, stapled. The envelope was licked and sealed. I call this solution the Fortune Cookie Principle. It's the same one I seem to have to learn again and again each time my anxiety rises: *Do it now*!

AM I LOOKING AT MYSELF HONESTLY?

What Would A Grown-up Do?

The 43rd Day

When I make a serious decision, I want to make it a good one that carries my life forward in a positive way. The alternative is to stick with my usual, outmoded method: I gallop in with a snap decision and pick up the pieces later, at my leisure. Not the most intelligent behavior, and time-consuming! I don't want the old ways any more. I need a *mind-stopper*, something to make me say "Whoa!" to myself before I plow in again.

Many people count to ten. I wanted a more practical mind-stopper, because counting made me pause, all right, but my head was filled with numbers rather than the problem at hand. Now I ask myself, "What would a grown-up do?" Mature people seem to have a good grasp on when to speak up, when to remain silent or step back, when to take action — and when to split! It's not easy to come by this wisdom. Some young people have it, while some old-timers don't, so it's evidently not just a matter of time on the planet. Besides, what's appropriate for you may not be right for me, so I can't just plug in "the answer"; it's important to find new answers that work well in *my* life.

I ask myself, "What would a grown-up do?" and then I imagine my most mature friends in my position. (Not the stuffy ones — the happy ones.) How would *they* proceed if faced with the same situation? My mind begins to focus on the decision-making *process* rather than an emotional response. I can study alternatives; I may even discover a more creative direction. Although I've always been open to adventure, now I'm more likely to have enough gas in the tank or a warm blanket for that unexpected night on the mountain.

Too much spontaneity is one of the reasons cats have nine lives. I only have one. It's getting more exciting and productive, now that I'm wasting less time in backtracking from poor decisions and have fewer pieces to pick up!

NOTES

I AM THANKFUL

THE 44th DAY

Sitting on my porch, I catch a flash of color and a whir of wings near the hanging basket of flowers. I don't breathe! The iridescent green hummingbird is hovering within a foot of my face . . . and at last I whisper a "Thank You."

I observe an elderly man helping an old woman to her seat; they are warm with each other, smiling . . .

I look out my taxi window; a purple and gold sunset is gloriously reflected on the glass wall of a skyscraper . . .

I'm feeling lonely when the phone rings. It is an old friend I need so much to share with . . .

My orange kitten, Punkin, bounces down the stairs to greet me, making joyful little talking noises . . .

I am writing; several good pages flow effortlessly from my pen . . .

The great shoulders of the Delaware Water Gap loom ahead of me on Route 80, as ever drawing me to them, welcoming me home . . .

. . . and I say "Thank You."

Surrounded by and immersed in the gifts of my Higher Power, the Creator of the Universe, I am delighted by the smallest things. As I become more conscious of wonders and beauties, I remember to say "Thank You" — sometimes out loud. More often I silently acknowledge that all things come from Him. I think of this as a daily spiritual activity that is essential to my well-being. Through this constant recognition, I assure myself of "an attitude of gratitude." At one time in my life, I would have brushed aside such a phrase as corny. Now it is the foundation of my life!

NOTES

THE 45th DAY

It's taken me a long time to realize what I need for my mental health: support and caring, attention and sharing — every day. I need all those positive strokes that let me know I'm okay, and keep my mind in reality. Now that I'm living alone, my daily need for people has become even more evident. My thinking gets screwy when the only mind I have to bounce ideas off of is my own!

My daily contacts can't be limited to business acquaintances, no matter how accommodating. The business world tends to wear masks of self-image and position. I must have honest friends who need the same human things of me that I need from them. I talk to these people face to face whenever I can, but some of my special friends have moved long distances recently: Rhode Island, Arizona, Virginia. That's okay. I think of my large phone bill as good mental medicine.

My grandmother used to write at least one letter every day, sending her long, chatty notes all over the country. She was still writing the week she died at ninety-four. When I was little I used to wonder what she could possibly have to say. Now I understand that the subject matter wasn't so important; she simply gave of herself, her happiness, grief, catastrophes — daily living.

I need to convey the same simple message: "I'm here. I care. I'm glad you're there."

NOTES

Loving In The Now

THE 46th DAY

It dawned on me one day that attention and love, if not identical, are inextricably connected. The amount of attention I bestow on someone is a clear measure of how much I care. I don't mean single-minded concentration. The only worthwhile attention is in the *now*, in that microsecond of consciousness that blends *all* the senses. It's a letting go of self and will; I become a sponge soaking up every nuance and vibration. It's a profoundly intimate moment.

How do I usually behave? My friend and I are in a heated discussion. As she speaks, my mind is planning a brilliant rebuttal — and my head is in the future. I can't respond fully to *her* at all. And if she plans her own points while I'm speaking, we never enter a dialogue; we merely alternate monologues! Where's my attention? Only on me. Evidently I'm giving my love to my own intellect and image.

The intimacy of *now* is most empowering in my relationship with my love. That first ecstasy of being *in love* is always joyously in the present. Every sense is heightened; ego boundaries soften and intertwine. We are accepting; we can do no wrong. Reality is suspended. Our relationship is permeated with thrilling, exhilarating sensuality. But that first burst of chemistry doesn't last; it couldn't possibly! Its purpose is to strengthen *bonding*, which can lead to a deeper, permanent relationship. Ideally, being *in* love gradually transforms into loving, or else it fades slowly and disappears.

If I want my commitment and bonding to grow, I must remain *in the present* with my love. He's not the perfect Prince Charming — but then, I'm no Cinderella either. I can fantasize a prince if I want to; fantasizing is common practice and there's nothing wrong with it. But if I indulge in fantasy *I'm consciously and willfully removing myself from his presence.* The more complete the fantasy, the more removed I become, until I no longer have any true sensual or sexual experience of him at all. It's all second-hand! Eventually I'll lose interest entirely, because my attention has been on my own fantasy instead of my real love. Why in heaven's name would I set myself a course that's *guaranteed* to carry me away from him? Calling upon a fantasy is the opposite of intimacy. Indeed, fantasy destroys intimacy.

NOTES ___

No Such Thing As Try

THE 47th DAY

When I first learned there was no such thing as "try," that it was just plain one-hundred-percent contrary to fact, I was flabbergasted! I had expended such mental energy in trying: to be a "good girl," to do it *right*, to behave, to show my parents, my friends, my boss and eventually my husband what pure motives I had. What did I just write? *Pure motives?* Uh-oh! This concept of "try" is already taking on a dimension I hadn't expected!

> I tried to remember your anniversary . . .
> I tried to get you a birthday present . . .
> I tried to get home on time . . .
> I tried to finish the project . . .

Who was I kidding? All these were said with sincerity and anguish. Have you noticed that the implied word following each of these phrases is "but"? Am I *pretending to be responsible*? Is "try" just a way to save face, to look good while I'm not following through? Ouch!

There's no such thing as try. If you've never gone through the obvious demonstration with someone, let me walk you through it now. Put this book down. Now try to pick it up. No, no. Don't actually pick it up—just *try*. Again, no. I don't want you just to leave it on the table! Of course you get the point; there is no *try*. You either *do* it or you *don't*! And if I nailed the book to the table, and the table to the floor, it wouldn't change a thing. You still either do it or you don't.

Once I removed this mealy-mouthed, irresponsible, face-saving word from my vocabulary, I immediately became more honest with myself, and with you. It's raised my self-esteem, because I'm more nearly who and what I say I am.

No fooling! My actions now speak for me. If I want to do something, I get it done. If it isn't yet completed, I can probably tell you when it will be; and if I don't wish to do it, I don't lie — I don't "try."

NOTES

ATTACH FEET TO MOUTH

THE 48th DAY

It's true that talk is cheap. I've always known I'd say just about anything to manipulate *you* into action. It's a lot easier than getting responsible for my own behavior. I'd threaten or cajole, promise or pretend, protest that "I can't stand this!" — and then settle down to tolerate it all a little longer. That's crazy! And I'm finally able to admit it.

Lately I've taken the time to observe and listen to myself with some honesty. When I'm ready to make a statement, I determine the truth of it *before* I open my mouth, by asking myself, "What's the action that goes with the statement? Attach feet to mouth!" No, I don't mean foot-in-mouth disease, those embarrassing remarks I fervently wish I'd never uttered. I'm talking about telling the truth. *When my actions don't match my words, then I'm lying to you.* (That's not too strong a statement. I refuse to minimize the seriousness of this behavior any longer. I'm either telling the truth or I'm not.)

People listen only to actions. Kids and spouses are especially good at this. They wait for me to act, and if I don't, they don't. Simple. As a mother I became a screamer; as a wife I became a martyr. The best way out of this dilemma is to be certain my requests or demands have an action attached that *I* can carry out. If I want the kitchen sink fixed and nothing happens after an appropriate time, I can fix it myself or call the plumber. If I'm living with an active alcoholic, once I've told him he's dangerous when he drives drunk, I must see to it that if he's been drinking I never drive with him again. I either drive, find another way to travel or don't go at all. Saying it isn't enough; I must also act. If I mete out punishment to one of my children, I need to do what I said I would, or not say it to begin with. Attach feet to mouth; suit the action to the words. Anything less is simply a lie. Words and actions together have the power of truth — and only then do I become a credible and trustworthy adult.

NOTES

Feel Guilty, Just Don't Act On It

The 49th Day

I believe there are several kinds of guilt. The distinctions can be confusing, because all guilt feels equally rotten, but some kinds of guilt need to be ignored or rethought and set aside. A trusted friend can help us with some honest evaluation.

The most significant guilt is my conscience at work, reminding me when I violate my own moral standards. The only way to avoid that guilt is not to perform the offending act. But there's a connected guilt that needs analysis; it's the guilt I feel when I *think* about performing that act. For example, I admire a spectacular piece of jewelry, and think how easy it would be to pocket it. Zap! comes the guilt. But I'm berating myself without cause; I haven't stolen since I was ten, and don't intend to begin now. Didn't someone say there'd be nobody left on the streets if we were jailed for thoughts as well as deeds? To remove that guilty feeling, I just remind myself I don't do that kind of thing.

Then there's "guilt by association." It's the sinking feeling I have when a friend gets in trouble — and I wasn't even around! I don't understand it, but I know it happens to me, and it happens especially to young people who are just developing their own moral codes and standards. Thinking it through reduces that kind of guilt to a mere whisper.

There's also the guilt that comes when I break the rules I was brought up by, even though the restrictions may no longer be appropriate. I feel a twinge when I don't wear black to a funeral, for example. A more severe form has to do with challenging traditional roles. A woman is particularly susceptible to agonies of guilt when she breaks free. Seeking a divorce comes to mind, or taking a battering husband to court. Although she's protecting her dignity and integrity as a human being, she may feel disloyal and guilty. Is it sometimes necessary to choose between guilt and self-esteem or self-protection? Yes, often that seems to be the choice. Better to opt for self!

A more insidious guilt is the one brought on by manipulation: "If you loved me . . ." sends off a warning signal in my head. Here comes my guilt, despite my certainty that I *don't want to do* what I'm being maneuvered into doing! Paying off a kid's parking ticket is a small, instructive example. Making decisions under emotional pressure (let's call it by its true name: blackmail) is miserable. When my conviction is doing battle with my guilt, it's usually because I'm going against a social role such as "loyal employee" or "good mother." Time to analyze the situation with a supportive friend because the role — and therefore the guilt — *may not be in my own best interest!*

WHAT ACTIONS DID I TAKE THIS WEEK?
WERE THEY GOOD FOR <u>ME</u>?

Enough Careers For A Lifetime

THE 50th DAY

Human beings are amazingly adaptable; we can function almost anywhere and do almost anything. We can make sticks and stones into useful tools or work with sophisticated instruments under a microscope. That's why I always get a sick feeling when I hear someone say, "I haven't been trained for anything else" or "I've only done one job in my life." What a negative way to think! Each of us tries out several *hundred* jobs in a lifetime. A few of them are truly appealing, and if we're smart we transform those interests into a career or two. Just off the top of my head, I can remember being a horse groomer, stable hand, actress, folk song writer, stage set designer, babysitter, goose feeder, seamstress, artist, hockey player, camp counselor, disc jockey, house painter (inside and out), sailor, baby nurse, lover, housewife, hostess, shop clerk, pet trainer, alcoholism counselor, chauffeur, typist, file clerk, accountant, bureaucrat, politician, treatment program designer, administrator, fundraiser, lecturer, workshop trainer, group leader, layout artist, cover designer, interior decorator, cook, dishwasher, architect, writer, editor and publisher. (No, I haven't done them all well, but I've tried each one. Some I loved; some I hated.) Each of these jobs had other jobs within it. It's an old and not so funny joke that if a housewife were adequately reimbursed for *each* of her skills she'd have a great résumé and a good paycheck.

I've often heard it said that I can be anything I want to be. Just about anyone can become a millionaire, for example. You simply invest ten percent of every single dollar that ever crosses your palm (including birthday money from your grandmother!). Millionaire status is almost inevitable by the time you reach fifty. Really. But there's a catch: your willingness and single-mindedness must be so complete that when you earn that dollar and you want a 92-cent ice cream cone you forego it, because you'd be two cents short of your ten percent for the millionaire's kitty!

I like to think that anyone can have a minimum of three to five careers in a lifetime. I've still got a lot of choices, so I don't want to wedge myself into a rut to rot. Within a few honest limitations, I believe it's absolutely true that I can be anything I want to be. I want to keep my options open. Now that I'm over fifty, it's not too likely that I'll become an Olympic gold medal swimmer. (For one thing, I don't like to get my face wet.) But I've always liked politics. Being a Senator isn't *totally* out of the question if I start *this very minute* and set my eye on becoming a precinct captain by fall. I want to learn everything from the local level on up. Will you vote for me? I think I'll start making plans!

NOTES

Make Waves

The 51st Day

I used to rant and rave over the many things that "should be done" that no one was doing, wasting a lot of anger and energy, until I came upon this saying:

> I asked, "Why doesn't somebody do that?"
> Then I realized, "*I'm* somebody!"

Can one person make a difference? Is it possible to fight City Hall? Can you accomplish the impossible dream? Damn right, you can! Every single thing that mankind has ever accomplished, for good *or* evil, has come about because one person had a vision and took a risk with singleness of purpose. There are a few simple steps you can take (notice I say simple, not easy!).

1. **Visualize your dream.** Say you want to start a manufacturing company. Imagine the whole process in concrete terms, from gathering information to working late nights, writing a proposal, convincing partners, designing a quality product, starting out in a drafty garage, and so on. Walk your mind through this lengthy process, knowing it will take months and maybe years. Did you begin your vision sitting lordlike behind an enormous desk directing everything? Then forget it!

   But perhaps you know you're not an idea person. Find one who is. A friend who stuck with me throughout the four years it took several of us to open a halfway house for women alcoholics put it beautifully: "You have ideas like butterflies constantly floating from your mind. My job is to grab my trusty butterfly net, catch a few beauties and bring them to earth." So she held onto the very same dream and made it happen through bookkeeping, painting, repairs and solid organization. Both talents were indispensable.

2. **Put the plan on paper.** Include ideas, needs, timetable, the pros and cons of the venture. If you must write a grant or proposal to acquire the necessary capital, you'll be forced to make it concrete. Even if it's your own money and you're going it alone, this process is necessary.

3. **Bring together enthusiastic support.** If your idea makes sense and you've visualized it well, your natural enthusiasm will carry others along with you. Although it's true that committees often design camels, more than one mind expands the number of possibilities and viable alternatives.

4. **Consult the necessary professionals.** You don't need to do it all alone. In fact, it's unwise. Honestly letting go of a piece of the power and creativity will allow you to accept and draw upon others' talents and skills. The bigger the project, the earlier they need to come on board.

5. **Become single-minded.** An enormous amount of your time and energy are needed. If you're not willing to contribute weekends, holidays and sleepless nights to the cause, what kind of commitment do you have? What attitude are you imparting to others? At the same time, you must avoid burnout at all costs. A fascinating dilemma!

6. **Have a partner or confidant.** You're going to feel depressed and hopeless at times. The "doubters" will circle like vultures, so it's best to have another firm believer at your side. The trick is to avoid having both of you falter at the same time. Alternating days of doubt is okay.

7. **Persevere.** This goes along with Number Six, keeping your spirits high and believing in the outcome no matter what. The race has always belonged to the turtle, not the hare. The race simply takes as long as it takes; keep on plodding!

Because of this philosophy, I've started several things that needed starting. Although the original concept was mine, I immediately called upon a number of dedicated and talented people to accomplish the mission together. The risk and fear are reduced and the enthusiasm is multiplied. I consider myself mainly the catalyst and cheerleader. As I write, an in-patient treatment center for alcoholic teenagers has just opened in northern New Jersey. It's taken six years for the dream to bear fruit. That's a long time, but it's a very big project. It's like starting a fifty-bed hospital, requiring tons of energy and hundreds of thousands of dollars. (Fund-raising is such fun, and so frustrating!) It's been necessary to beat off the doubters and constantly re-lift the banner of the dream. But oh, is the effort worthwhile! Hundreds, perhaps thousands, of young people will have another chance at this marvelous, ephemeral, wonderful life, enhanced by the powerful philosophy of the Twelve Steps and the loving fellowship of Alcoholics Anonymous.

NOTES

THE CAROUSEL CURE

THE 52nd DAY

I was feeling restless and irritable and vaguely dissatisfied — a search-for-meaning kind of feeling that I needed to analyze. At last I recognized it: merry-go-round withdrawal! For me, this is an insidious, chronic disease that slowly builds in tension over several months. It's the result of unrelieved adulthood, of tending only to duties and not to the little me inside. It means I haven't enjoyed plain old *fun*, laughing and giggling and blowing bubbles. I've avoided looking foolish and feeling free. I've been taking myself seriously. *Too* seriously!

I'm an addictive rider. No one is more rapturous than I when the tinkly music starts and the horse begins its slow, voluptuous surge forward. I'm a kid again! When did I ever stop being one? And wonder of wonders, H.P. has planned ahead again for my benefit. He's placed a merry-go-round just ten miles from my new home. It isn't the kind with moving horses, but that's okay. It's a merry-go-round and it's waiting for me.

Hey! I'm going for a ride on the merry-go-round. A friend just my age is going with me. I can't wait, I'm so excited! I always run for the outside horse, because it goes much farther than all the rest. My father taught me that. I may be the only grown-up surreptitiously stroking the nose of my gleaming pony. Will I look foolish? Who cares! I'm taking good care of myself.

Want to come too?

NOTES

WHAT DO I WANT?

THE 53rd DAY

For all my early life, I followed the rules as I understood them — doing my best to be a "good girl" and please other people, particularly family. I was what I was supposed to be, did what I was supposed to do and even thought what I was supposed to think. I had no way, then, of knowing that much of my hostility came from acting in ways that were contrary to my basic nature.

When I began to get sober, someone asked me what *I* wanted to do in a certain situation. I was astonished. I don't believe I'd ever asked that question of myself in just that way. It had always been what was I *supposed* to do, based on the power other people had over me and my decisions. I didn't know I could make decisions based on my own self-interest. I didn't even know what *was* in my interest! "What do I want to do?" was a brand-new concept. Later I was fascinated to realize that seeking a divorce was actually the very first decision I'd ever made *just for myself.* Heady stuff! It was also a lonely place to be.

"What do *I* want?" is a question that comes in two forms. One form really asks me what I *desire* or *need* — materially, socially, philosophically, emotionally. The other is action-oriented and self-responsible: what do I want to *do* in a given situation. (I know immediately I'm on the wrong track if my sentence starts with, "I want *him* to . . .")

So I ask myself the question several times a day, with the emphasis on "I". It's marvelous for dealing with salesmen and spouses and kids, all of whom may be maneuvering me into a position contrary to my own best interests. Asking myself the question slows me down momentarily and gives me a little time for analysis. It gives me the chance to unhook from "Let me do what pleases them" or "What would a *good* mother do?" I may indeed end up doing what pleases them, but it will please me first! I now know that what I want isn't always popular, but that's just the point, isn't it? "Popular" implies "people-pleasing" again.

Is this what they call self-determination? You bet it is!

NOTES

IF IT AIN'T BROKE, DON'T FIX IT

THE 54th DAY

I have a hard time accepting and enjoying peace and serenity. Once my little world is purring smoothly, I start getting edgy — looking around for something to manipulate and change. My old boss once said, "Judy, you can stir things up without opening your mouth." Since I've yet to keep my mouth shut in my whole life, I know he was exaggerating. But the fact is, I get an overwhelming urge to *stir the pot*, just to watch it steam and bubble. Any change will do, just so it's different from whatever's going on right now. This frenetic behavior produces a mood change in me, just as alcohol once did. Five minutes of relative calm and watch out; I'm at it again!

Some people seem to be hooked on excitement or addicted to the rush of adrenaline. This may be part of the explanation. My family were New Englanders, however, and I was brought up in a low-key, sedate and well-regulated home. There were few fights; voices were seldom raised; careful plans were meticulously executed. This methodical upbringing is probably one source of my impatience, having taught me to anticipate total control over my environment — dominion over people, places and things.

Entering a room for the first time, I often spend a few moments of mental rearrangement: moving furniture, repainting and papering, imagining new artwork and bric-a-brac. It's partly an overactive feminine decorating trait, but most of all I have a need to *manage* my surroundings. In the same vein, I sit in the same chair each week at meetings, get irritated if we don't start on time when I'm not the leader, and so on. This is surely control of the most basic variety, irritating to others and frustrating to me.

It doesn't matter why this behavior began; I'm changing it. I'm striving instead for acceptance of my surroundings: people as they are, places as they lie, things as they sit. *If it ain't broke, don't fix it* is such a delightful way to put it. Accept life on life's terms, yes? How difficult for me, breaking a lifetime habit of take-charge-control. It's good discipline. I've become more observant. Sometimes I'm even able to admit that other ways are just as good as my ways. (I'm not yet able to admit they might be better!) This has brought me to a revolutionary idea: *Tolerance is a mood-changer, too!*

NOTES

THE 55th DAY

"God, grant me the *serenity* to accept the things I cannot change, *courage* to change the things I can, and *wisdom* to know the difference." (Italics mine)

Reinhold Niebuhr, whose prayer this is, wrote several other verses, but these four deceptively simple lines are what capture the imagination. Emblazoned on plaques and mugs, cards and keychains, this prayer is so familiar that its message may be overlooked. Like any profound idea, it means different things to each of us as our circumstances change and our lives evolve.

I was thirty-five when I first came upon the Serenity Prayer. I had never developed a personal relationship with God, having had only a vague sense of Him as a distant creator. My early life was neither introspective nor philosophical. When I recognized my need for fundamental change, I was drawn to the prayer's simple, powerful message.

Niebuhr says that *serenity, courage* and *wisdom* are gifts granted by God, not gained through my own efforts. My intellect, then, is not the motivating force. Instead, my willingness to ask for and accept these gifts is *my* part of the bargain. The moment I repeat this prayer sincerely, it becomes an implicit contract between my God and me; this process of giving and receiving is a partnership. (I'm still puzzled by the implication that acceptance comes *as a result* of God-given serenity; I thought it must be the reverse. It may be years before I comprehend it.)

This is what the prayer says to me:

I ask for *serenity* so that I can accept life on God's terms — people, places, things; death, destruction, aging and other losses.

I ask for *courage* so that I can take self-responsible action (changing is hard on the ego, which must give way!).

I ask for *wisdom* to determine what it is I really have power over. It would seem the answer is me, only *me*.

So I see this as a very *action*-oriented prayer, and the title may be misleading. I set the action in motion by the simple process of asking, then the two of us can work together on *me*. At least I don't have to do it alone.

Changing myself is very hard work indeed. I know instinctively that it's a lifetime proejct heaped with setbacks and reversals. I dread the very idea of it! Is it worth the effort? Am *I* worth the effort? The Serenity Prayer contract must be renewed in some form every single day. When I renew it wholeheartedly, I continue the journey toward a contentment and peace beyond anything I can imagine. I believe this is so — and it's so simple. Now, if I can only get my know-it-all ego to take a back seat . . .

Worry Is A Waste Of Energy

The 56th Day

Worry and self-pity are kissing cousins. Worry has a similar sick satisfaction to it, because once again it's possible to play the role of Unique One, focusing, even if miserably, on me, me, *me*. It may even have a touch of overblown ego to it: "If I can't be the best, I can at least be the most burdened!"

Worry is clearly a *learned* mental habit, near kin to biting your nails or twisting a lock of hair (both of which go well with worry). Some people have it and some don't. My family never taught me the lousy luxury of worry, although my brother was a master at it, spending many a fine, sleepless night. I used to tell him that worry is made stronger through practice and repetition, and that *worry can be unlearned*. The most important step is willingness — being willing to let go of all that exciting turmoil. If you're ready, here are several tried-and-true steps you can take. With regular practice, they will eventually remove worry from your life.

1. Buy a bedside Worry Book. If you consider yourself a champion worrywart, you may opt for a leather-bound ledger, but any solid notebook with lots and lots of empty pages will do.
2. Artfully designate the first page "My Worries," and sign it with a flourish. Ritual always makes one feel better. Then label the second page "Worry One" and give it a title. You may wish to start with a minor worry and leave the sanity-threatening ones for later, after you've made some progress in worry reduction.
3. Now describe the breadth and depth of the worry in detail, as objectively as you can and without emotion.

Use as many pages as you need.

4. Label the next page "Feelings About Number One" and exhaust that category.
5. The following page is "Conclusions and Options" and includes possible actions to resolve the worry.
6. The next page is "People to Call" and contains a list of knowledgeable friends and professionals.
7. The last page is the "Worst Case Scenario," or simply "WCS." Here you write starkly and boldly the very worst outcome you've imagined. The bottom line is reserved for your answer to the question: "Can I accept this?" Only a "yes" or "no" is appropriate.

I'm not by nature a worrier, being far too lazy to expend so much psychic energy on wheel-spinning and "what ifs." But I have found myself sleepless a few times. Out comes the notepad so I can move the worry from my head to the paper. This is the most significant step, usually taking less than fifteen minutes (note again the similarity to self-pity). I'm able to sleep once I've promised myself to reread the worry, the feelings, the options and the contacts, the WCS *and* my willingness to accept it — over my first cup of morning coffee. It looks different in the sunlight! It looks less daunting and intimidating on paper!

After the second cup of coffee, I put the *whole* list of people to call on my "must do" agenda for the day. (See the Fortune Cookie Principle on page 95.) With this process I can go from worry to action to relief.

AM I WORKING ON MYSELF?
AM I DOING WHAT I WANT?

THE 57th DAY

Once upon a time I said "yes" for all the wrong reasons:

I said "Yes, I'll do that" when I didn't want to — or even when it wasn't good for me — because I *should.*

I said "Yes, I'll do that for you" when I didn't want to — just so you'd like me.

I said "Yes, I believe this, or I like that" even when I didn't — just so I'd fit into the group.

But the one thing I couldn't do was to say "Yes, that's me" when you accused me of something. I don't mean when you accused me falsely. Oh, no! I mean when you accused me of something that was *true* of me, but didn't suit my image of myself. Maybe it was the tone of voice that got me. Or maybe it wasn't your intention to accuse, but simply to confront, and I automatically reacted negatively. I'd come back at you with a hundred defenses and justifications, pushing you away without even bothering to check on the truth of your statement. You see, I was afraid to be wrong, and afraid to hear the truth. Strangely, I was afraid because I thought that *whatever I was must be permanent*. I didn't learn about the possibility of changing myself until I was in my thirties. Such a slow learner!

Now I've become willing to listen to your comments (although I must admit that I still brace myself inside!). At least I no longer rush to man the defenses. Instead, no matter what your tone of voice, I pause to ask myself, "Is this so? Am I really that way?" And if I'm being honest with myself (which is difficult) and my answer to myself is *yes*, then I say "Yes, that's true" to you. Nobody can manipulate me through my own guilt or my need to people-please if I already know the truth about myself. And, at the same time, I'm beginning to set aside my old self-image and getting at the real me.

So this is my new rule: *Don't defend yourself against the truth. Acknowledge it; say yes!*

NOTES

SAY *NO*

THE 58*th* *DAY*

Once upon a time I said "no" only out of stubbornness.

I didn't say "no" when I wanted to, or even when it would have been good for me — because I thought I shouldn't. I didn't want you to think I was selfish.

I didn't say "No, I won't do that for you" even when I wanted to — because I thought you wouldn't like me.

I didn't say "No, I don't believe this, or I don't like that" — even when it was so — just so I'd fit into the group.

But I finally discovered it was *imperative* that I say "no" and stick to it. I was sick of living a lie. To my surprise, the sky didn't fall in the first time I said "no." My friends remained my friends; my boss didn't fire me. Instead, it proved to be the quickest way to raise my self-esteem. I began to respect myself because I was stating my position honestly.

The second thing I learned was, "No, with no frills." No explanations or excuses were necessary. "No," it seems, is a complete sentence all by itself. Besides, I was sure to give some weak argument if I began to explain myself, and a good manipulator could leap in with all four feet. Best to leave it at "no." Facing further argument, I learned I could keep my mouth shut (!) and just shake my head.

Then I learned that true unselfishness comes *as the result of prior selfishness*. I'm free to say "yes" once I'm absolutely certain I can say "no" for my own protection any time I desire. "Yes" becomes a clear choice rather than an abject capitulation caused by guilt or the need to please other people. I can say "yes" out of caring and concern. It seems a paradox that the surest way to become unselfish is to learn to say ''no'' in the most selfish way!

NOTES ____________________

THE 59th DAY

It's amazing how anxiety and apprehension well up in me whenever I *think* of making major changes in my life — moving, for example, or shifting jobs — even when the decision is totally under my control. Take a simple plan to fast for the day; near panic floods over me! I used to believe these feelings were way out of proportion to the action I was contemplating.

A friend suggested a simple experiment designed to teach me how stressful change really is. I was to observe myself carefully as I dressed each morning — whether pants went on before shirt, which arm or leg went first, and did I put on the left shoe before the right, or vice versa? Once I knew my pattern, *I was to change the order of dressing totally.* Whatever was usual, I was to do the exact opposite. Talk about crazy-making! Well into the afternoon of that day I was still irritable and anxious, unable to think clearly, head in a whirl — all from making a conscious decision to change the way I put on my clothes!

It was an important lesson. It's a simple fact that making changes of any kind is a source of real discomfort. Add to that a change in my approach to *people* and my anxiety skyrockets. Perhaps I need to be more understanding of myself; perhaps I'm merely being human!

I decided I must give myself a little emotional leeway, a method of easing into new behaviors more gently. A month of *maybe* turns out to be the ideal solution:

"Maybe you're right" is a fine answer to a confrontation.

"Maybe I will; I'll let you know" is a good response to a demand.

"Maybe" still buys me a few weeks while I plan new behaviors. Allowing myself more time than that would give me room to slither out from under my self-responsibility. (My anxiety also increases when I know I'm waffling.) So after a month of "maybe," I'm ready to give it up, but that little kindness to myself really works.

NOTES

WHEN IN DOUBT, DON'T

THE 60th DAY

Good decision-making is a skill perfected over many years. It weighs pros and cons and predicts probable results; it takes into account hunches and feelings and other subtleties. But when a small flag of doubt flutters through the back of my mind, I promptly stomp on it so that what I want to do prevails. My style is to make grandiose snap decisions and then step back to see how many other shoes will drop! So it's hard for me to accept that little flag as a legitimate warning. It represents many nebulous ideas and experiences, important clues that gently demand recognition. I need to say to myself, "Stop! All the facts aren't in. Something in my complex computer-brain isn't in accord with my conscious decision. Trust the computer; wait a while."

The other subtle signal is my own procrastination. Perhaps I haven't been following through on the details of some plan, even though my intellect tells me it's brilliant. Time to analyze my putting-off performance. Since procrastination is one of my strongest character defects, I have to be especially honest with myself. Am I stalling, or is it a subconscious, niggling knowledge that I would be wise not to proceed in that direction?

"When in doubt, don't" is not a license to abdicate responsibility. If your usual method is to stall on everything, stop reading this page and go straight on to "You Can't Win if You're Not in the Game" (page 141). The ideas on *this* page are for the too-spontaneous, jump-in-with-both-feet sorts of people, and the message is: pause and re-evaluate. Why not lay out the problem and get feedback from trusted friends or professionals? I may run the alternatives through my imagination once again to see how they feel. If I have no more doubts after an honest re-evaluation, then I say to myself, ''Go for it!'' There's nothing more thrilling than getting a new project under way, but it's all the more satisfying if it's well planned and skillfully executed.

NOTES

You Can't Win If You're Not In The Game

THE 61st DAY

'Tis better to have loved and lost,
Than never to have loved at all.

Nothing ventured, nothing gained.

Do I have to throw those old truisms at myself to get motivated? I've heard them all, and I believe every one. I know that risking is the difference between merely *getting by* and really *living*. But I'm still mired in the old habit patterns of my upbringing: intellectual, proper, reserved. Do you know how hard it is for me to say "I need a hug"?

My intellectual self needs to lay out alternatives. The first thing I know is that *not* risking has one result: *nothing happens*. Risking means taking some kind of positive action *without being certain of the results*. There are four possible outcomes.

Relationships	**Business**
I may be rejected	Bankruptcy!
I may be misunderstood;	Business declining
Nothing will change	No new production or profit
New levels of love.	Economic boom!

Two of the four possibilities give me status quo or better. Bankruptcy and rejection aren't all that likely, and "better" means increased profits or improved self-esteem, trust, intimacy, honesty and deepening love. Great. I'm willing to take a risk. Why this year more than last year? It just came to me one day, with all the immediacy and power of a new insight: *this is the only life I have*. Before it's too late, I intend to make it *the best*.

So I may lose it all. Or my life may just plod along — but it may get light-years better. In fact, I'm expecting it. I'll risk being honest about *me*, and choose the best opportunities that come my way. The results may not always be what I envision, but that's okay. This is it! I'm in the game!

NOTES

ONE HUNDRED PERCENT ONE WAY

THE 62rd DAY

Whenever there's a problem between two people, it usually boils down to a lack of sharing, but the excuse is, "*He* doesn't communicate with *me*!" Delving a little further, we hear that "I don't bother to talk with him any more, because *he* won't communicate." So who's stopped? If I explain that good communication is one hundred percent one-sided — that it's all up to *me* — I get an immediate, vehement protest: *It's got to be fifty-fifty!*

The fact is, I can only manage myself. I have no control whatsoever over someone else, either how he hears me or how he responds. Hey, I wish I did! When we were first married, I would wail at my stubborn second husband, "You never listen to me!" And he would answer me (not even smugly, just seriously), "I hear every word you say. You're bitching because I don't jump to do everything you want." I was furious! How dare he hit so close to the truth! But he started me thinking about what I could expect from him; eventually I realized I must limit my expectations to myself. Adequate, honest communication is one hundred percent up to me.

I even spelled out an ideal checklist. If everyone communicated this way, what a glorious world we'd live in! Can I follow it perfectly? Of course not. No one can.

Express feelings — using "I am" sentences.

Be honest — even if it shows me in a negative light.

If I'm wrong, promptly admit it.

Avoid accusatory "you" statements — stick to complimentary ones.

Be factual — tell the truth without minimizing.

Modulate my tone of voice — no pity or sarcasm.

Be brief — no nagging repetition.

Stick to the subject — no dragging up the past.

State what I need — but don't make demands.

Don't threaten — but do follow through.

Accept the other person's right to a contrary opinion.

Listen — and respond accordingly.

If I don't understand, check it out: "Do you mean . . .?"

Compromise circumstances — not self or standards.

Check my motives.

Don't expect the outcome to be *my* way.

See the humor of the situation.

One day my husband and I were having a dandy fight — and we were fighting *fair*! Suddently we looked each other in the eye and began roaring with laughter and hugging each other, because we knew at exactly the same moment that we couldn't remember the point of it all!

Yes, I still get angry and defensive. Sure I deny the truth. I threaten; I accuse; I want what I want when I want it. If I'm going to pay attention to my own checklist, my willingness must be one hundred percent, but it often isn't. The hardest thing to remember is that I have *zero control* over the other person. In the unlikely event that we're both doing our level best at the same time, the result is one hundred-one hundred, not fifty-fifty. It's true intimacy, and may occur about five whole minutes out of a month — and then only if we're truly committed and working hard at it.

THE TEN-SECOND CONFRONTATION

THE 63rd DAY

Sometimes a friend or spouse, co-worker, neighbor or workman simply *must* be confronted about some unacceptable behavior. It's probably the thing I hate most in all the world to do, so I used to spend a month or more marshalling my feelings and forces until I'd manufactured a deadly weapon. What did I accomplish? I vented a lot of resentment. The other person's response was predictable: at the very least, a stubborn wall of silence and resistance. Some people ducked and ran! Spouses gave me a vehement argument or brushed me off. I knew I had to confront, but my methods weren't working, so I decided to read up on the subject and analyze my circumstances. There had to be a better way!

What do I want a confrontation to accomplish? I want the other person to *hear* me, rather than build up immediate defenses. Since I know I can't change someone else, angry demands are out. I want to do all of the following: act like an adult, express how I feel, describe the negative behavior, and report what I'll do about it. A truthful confrontation means I must be willing *and prepared* to follow through. It sounds as if the whole thing might take less than ten seconds, doesn't it? And here I'd always prepared for a two-hour harangue!

A friend of mine has an obnoxious husband. He's a tasteless boor who's known for putting her down in public. She's a meek and gentle woman, so he could always do as he pleased. Besides, she admits she never really let him know how much she despised his behavior. Oh, maybe she'd protest feebly once in a great while so he could laugh and brush her off as merely "silly."

She was ready for major changes. We planned her confrontation carefully. It was masterful! We wrote and rewrote it, because we knew she'd have to rehearse. They were going to the home of friends one night, so we decided on these lines:

> "I feel embarrassed when you put me down in front of our friends. If you insult me tonight, I'll leave immediately."

Talk about powerful! Did her husband believe her? Of course not! How was he to know she was undoing fifteen years of abject passivity in one evening? Before she told him, she had to be sure she'd follow through. And she was positive, so we practiced the other line we suspected she'd need before the night was over:

> (To her friends) "Excuse me. I'm sorry, but I must leave now. I promised my husband I would never again put up with his insults." (Exit, front door)

She'd prepared herself with her own set of car keys, and money for a taxi if he kept her from using their car.

He didn't believe her; at dinner she was the butt of another tasteless joke. Yes, she was shaking all over when she stood up, spoke her piece and exited. Her husband was so stunned he didn't make any attempt to stop her. He had to ask someone for a ride home later, and felt appropriately humiliated. And he has never, ever insulted her again in public *or* in private. She has blossomed into a new and vibrant woman since that liberating night.

AM I WILLING TO BE HONEST AND COMMUNICATE ONE HUNDRED PERCENT?

The Formula Is $\frac{I}{E}$

The 64th Day

Feelings need to be recognized and appropriately expressed; we need to keep the negative ones from festering, and validate the positive ones. Letting others know what's happening inside us is part of honest, open communication. Besides, I need to pay attention to the subtleties of gut reactions, because they often get beneath my conscious rationalizations and move me closer to the truth.

As a society, however, we seem to have lost sight of the need for balance between thinking and feeling. I believe we've swung from over-intellectualization to over-emotionality, leaning too far toward "If it feels good, do it" and "Don't think; feel!" These ideas got me into a lot of trouble. They were the motivation behind my alcoholism. It's just plain *stinking thinking*, giving feelings dominance over good decision-making. Basing decisions on feelings alone is foolish, and can be very dangerous.

Perceptions and thoughts go before feelings, no matter how fleetingly or unrecognized. Emotional maturity depends upon good *thinking* habits and good *analyzing* skills learned over time. They result in good judgments. So I subscribe to the formula "I over E," meaning *intellect over emotions*. It's what I *think* that causes the feeling to begin with. (Yes, that's the fact, regardless of how much it seems to be the other way around.) And it's what I think or perceive about my feelings that matters, even if I don't put it all consciously into words. And finally, it's the *action* I take based on my thinking process that really counts.

"I'm in a difficult and unsatisfying job." (perception)

"I'm deeply depressed." (feeling)

''Feeling this way is not normal.'' (mature thinking)

''I'm calling a counselor for an appointment.'' (positive action)

''I'm in a difficult and unsatisfying job.'' (perception)

''I'm deeply depressed.'' (feeling)

''I can't *stand* to feel this way any longer!'' (stinking thinking)

''I'll take a little something to stop the pain.'' (self-destructive action)

In the second example, the result of immature thinking is poor judgment. This case could lead to addiction or suicide, because it's what I *think* about feeling depressed that matters. (And don't forget, it was what I *thought* about the job that got me depressed in the first place! If I'd decided the job was either satisfying or acceptable, I'd never have become depressed.)

Learning good thinking habits is the road to emotional maturity. I need to use the good, analytical brain I was given — to listen to friends, study alternatives, think actions through, accept consequences. Good decision-making leads to appropriate feelings and good judgments. *I don't just follow my feelings alone,* because they can get me into trouble; they're all too often the end-product and result of deluded thinking.

NOT TO DECIDE *IS* TO DECIDE

THE 65th DAY

When I keep putting something off, it may not be procrastination, but a decision I've already made and not yet admitted to myself. If I'm being honest, I let myself know:

I've decided not to do that (yet).

I've made a decision to table that (for a while).

I'm not ready to take action on that.

I'm just procrastinating. I'll get around to it (someday).

And sometimes, equally honestly: "I'm kidding myself. I'm *never* going to do that. Time to accept the fact."

I don't need to berate myself. Some decisions *need* to be put off for a while; perhaps a decision now would be premature and hasty. I'll make a better one after a period of reflection. New and necessary information is apt to show up in the intervening days — or I may have a change of attitude. Time frequently does that to attitudes.

If the decision concerns a relationship, I may attend several months of counseling first, with or without my partner.

If the decision is connected with grief, I may wait until the pain subsides and my head has become clearer.

If it's a business decision, I may wait for the quarterly financial report.

If I'm making a large purchase, I may save up the total price rather than buying on credit.

If it's not plain old procrastination, then I'll be able to give myself an honest *renegotiation* date. Right on my calendar I write "D-Day" for Decision Day. It may involve a serious subject like going back to school, buying a car, changing jobs or filing for divorce. The new decision may be to hire a professional, hash over the subject with a friend, drop the plan entirely — or legitimately postpone the decision for another few months as new information surfaces.

Once I have "D-Day" clearly in mind and emblazoned on the calendar, I can forget about it and unclutter my mind for a while. It's postponed, but not forgotten. For this process to work, I must be certain of my self-honesty. That's the real key! I need to know that it's an intelligent, considered postponement, not just procrastination. The pointless worrying and wheel-spinning cease only if I'm getting more mature in my behavior.

NOTES ____________________

THE 66th DAY

A friend visiting my house remarked, "I love what you've created for yourself." I like that. It gets to the heart of my philosophy. I create *everything* in my life. Where and how I place myself each moment *is* significant. I may chat cheerfully with strangers on the supermarket line, or clip their heels with my cart. I may choose to be drunk at a cocktail party, or spend that evening peacefully on the beach. I may rush tunnel-visioned through the crowd or stroll on the sunny side of the street.

Once upon a time I believed most things "just happened to me." Now I know that I choose every person, place and circumstance. I used to wolf my breakfast as I watched the morning news. Now I carry my plate to the front porch to enjoy the glint of early sunlight on the water. I've chosen a qualitatively different environment, internally and externally, though I've moved my body a mere seventeen feet.

I choose to live in drabness or beauty — and it has nothing whatever to do with money. My first marriage was surrounded by expensive antiques. When I married my second husband, I moved to a much more modest house. While I was painting the living room, my oldest son told me that he wanted me to decorate his home for him when he grew up. I could've chosen that time to give him a lecture on wives and mothers-in-law, taste and rivalry, but I was learning. Instead, I simply asked him why, and he said the most profound thing: "Because you decorate friendly." (And I'd been secretly chewing myself up inside because I couldn't afford a new sofa. How slow I am to learn!)

But "creating my environment" isn't just a Pollyanna philosophy for making the best of a bad deal. *I even create* the bad deal! Every turn I take, every choice I make, every job I accept (or reject, by my behavior at the interview), every argument for my limitations or for my talents sends me in a certain direction. *I have chosen where I am today.* Every past choice has led me to this place. To *exactly* this place. The smallest choices and the biggest ones, all combined to this end. In my life I create *this* person, *this* job, *this* house, *this* attitude, *this* bank account.

And you've created your exact place at this very moment, too. Why do you have this action-oriented, get-off-your-duff, you've-got-the-power book in your hands right now? Because you're willing to believe? Good heavens, I don't care what you *believe*! Just choose your *actions*. You don't like the environment you're in? Create a new one. The least expensive and most empowering step is to create a new, inner You. The rest comes as you learn to make more educated and creative choices. Is it really important whether you choose to gobble your lunch on the job, or take the sandwich outside to sit under the only tree in the parking lot? Are you more likely to get that raise or new position if you've taken a relaxing break and are making clear, incisive decisions?

You already know what I think.

One Of God's Creatures

The 67th Day

My ego has always been outsize, a not-so-fragile balloon of puffery and pretense that acts as a buffer between me and my vulnerability. It took years to get this protective shield in order, and I'd like to chip away at it slowly. Otherwise I get the feeling I might go *bang!* all at once.

All my important insights, the ones that deflate my ego, seem only to come after years of struggle and denial. The weight of new evidence finally forces home a change of attitude or perspective. I know when I've had a profound awakening because my head goes *Flash! Click!* and the new idea is firmly implanted.

Late one afternoon I sat on the grass watching the squirrels at play, while a line of ants carried larvae to a new sandhill. I was fascinated. I was becoming immersed in the intricacies of the natural word — which I had ignored for years — and reflecting on the fact that each creature has its role to play, from the tiniest insect to the greatest . . .

And there I was! Reduced in that moment to a creature of the universe, no longer a mistress in control, dictating events, the center of the system. Just another of God's creations, small and powerless but beautiful and perfect, with my own special role to play. The ant had no idea of the purpose of his universe. No more had I, but it was nevertheless profoundly satisfying. I was no longer an observer, but a participant. A wave of serenity drifted over me and settled inside. The worst of my interior battles was over. I had surrendered to the truth. I knew it.

That moment has never left me. When I get too rambunctious, controlling and self-centered, the experience comes unbidden to my mind: I am merely one of God's tiny creatures — and that is enough.

NOTES

MISERY IS OPTIONAL

THE 68th DAY

Lousy, sad, unfair, hurtful, rotten things happen. That's part of life, and I know I can't change it, but I like the tough little saying:

Pain is inevitable; misery is optional.

It's just another twist on the idea that "If I continue to be miserable, I must be doing something wrong." I said that recently to a friend whose lemon of a car was back in the shop for the fifth time. His pent-up anger exploded. "What do you mean, *I'm* doing something wrong? *They're* the idiots!" Of course all that anger was burning inside of *him*, not the mechanics at the shop. I pointed out that he was opting for misery instead of action, and I suggested he look at all the alternatives he might take instead of stewing. In no time at all we came up with several:

1. Call the company president.
2. Picket the dealer's house.
3. Take the shop to small claims court.
4. Bomb the dealership.
5. Invoke the Lemon Law.
6. Go on vacation.
7. Paint the car yellow and bury it (with T.V. coverage).
8. Borrow a bike.
9. Write the Better Business Bureau.
10. Buy a motorcycle.
11. Enjoy his newest exercise — walking.
12. Wait patiently until it's fixed and pay the bill gracefully.

13. Sell the damned thing and take the loss.

Sometimes the answer to impotent misery is action; sometimes it's acceptance of something I can't change. Misery is part of victimhood; in every single case I can opt for an alternative. I need to remember that!

NOTES

THE 69th DAY

Several years ago, I went through a six-month bout of depression. I didn't recognize it as such, but I remember spending much of every day methodically turning the pages of a magazine. I can't even tell you if I was holding it right side up! The children were heaven knows where; meals were miserably haphazard. I didn't care if I lived or died, but only vaguely realized something was wrong. I couldn't say, "Quick! Get me out of here. I can't help myself!" because I didn't know.

Now I do, because several years later I observed an extraordinarily loving act. A woman who recognized her friend's severe depression simply took charge. She broke into the friend's house, physically dressed her and forced her to take a walk, ignoring all protests. Then she called a doctor and drove her friend to the hospital. Much later we learned that there had been a full bottle of pills on the bedside table; that morning was to have been the day for her suicide.

Everyone gets depressed at one time or another. Is it caused by grief, disease, hopelessness, anger turned inward, alcohol or drugs, or body chemistry gone awry? Whatever the trigger, unchecked depression may become so severe that extensive therapy, medication and even hospitalization are necessary. By that time I surely won't be able to help myself; I'll be led passively away. But I want to be in charge of my own life! So I must be selfishly responsible for my own mental health, attending to down periods while they're still minor dips in my energy level, so they don't have a chance to catch hold and envelop me once again.

Do I feel like staying in bed today, pulling the blankets

over my head to avoid life? If I give in to that tiny feeling, I'm already admitting to myself that I'm refusing to take responsibility for the consequences of my depression. It's time to use my head: *Don't give in to that lethargy. Move!* Almost anywhere will do, so long as I shift physically from one spot to another. My daily attitude counteracts depression; the essays in this book give several suggestions. Most of all I stay in touch with positive friends who can hear a shift in my mood. And I set myself positive goals — goals I can manage, not impossible dreams that set me up for defeat. I plan to keep acting in my own best interest while I have a good intellectual sense of what's happening to me. Preventing depression is so much easier than climbing out of the bottomless pit of despair once I've allowed myself to tumble over the brink!

NOTES

Celebrate The Good Things

The 70th Day

Over the years my family expended enormous amounts of energy on negative, hurtful things, leaving precious little time for anything else. My two boys, perhaps because of this emphasis on the negative, took turns playing the role of "scapegoat." They were envious of the approval we gave to the "good little sister," but she swears she never got the attention either. I suppose the truth is somewhere in between — and in the eye of the beholder.

At that time my parental language reflected the down side. It was filled with "don't" and "no" and "wrong" because that's where my focus was. I wanted my kids to "grow up right" and I didn't know any better. My daughter, whose grades were consistently high, says I'd zero in on the lowest letter on the report card, rather than say to her, "Great! I'm proud of you!" Once I became aware of this constant nothing's-good-enough approach, I began to monitor my mouth. Much low self-esteem had already resulted. My husband and I discussed my behavior, and he helped me make some real inroads. We often ignored negative activities almost entirely, spotlighting the wonderful things in each of us instead. Before that time, I didn't know how to give a compliment, let alone receive one. I had to be taught.

* * *

I had been asleep almost an hour when my twenty-year-old son phoned. He was being detained by the police in some small town a good distance away, and wanted me to pick him up. I was surprised he'd even ask, because he knew my stand on making rescues involving irresponsible acts. I told him "no" and went back to sleep.

I'd planned a party for the next weekend. It was to be a graduation celebration for him and his sister and I was especially proud of him; he'd gone through a personal struggle and come out with flying colors, finally enrolling himself in college. I learned from his girlfriend that he had refused to come, because he was still angry with me for turning down the midnight rescue. When I finally reached him by phone, I urged him to come. The whole family would be there to show him how proud we were, because we wanted to celebrate the good things that were happening to him.

He stubbornly reiterated that I hadn't supported him when he asked for help, which was certainly true. What he said next made me laugh out loud. It has rung in my mind ever since: "That's the trouble with this family; we only celebrate the good things!" Did he know how profound his remark was? We had indeed (pretty much) given up putting energy into negative activities. We were concentrating on our family's good qualities instead.*

I devoutly wish I'd known how to celebrate the good things when my children were very young, but what's done is done. Regretting the past is pointless, unless I can make amends in the present. Today I believe my language reflects my new awareness: I find myself spontaneously saying things like "That's great! excellent; wonderful. I like that; it makes me feel good; terrific!" I think my kids are just now beginning to feel the difference.

---

*Sure, he came! He was the guest of honor!

HOW DO I CREATE MY OWN ENVIRONMENT?
IS MISERY MERELY OPTIONAL?

The Opposite Of Love

The 71st Day

As a young teenager I read *The Scarlet Letter,* identifying strongly with the pain of the punishment inflicted on Hester Prynne. Imagine walking down the main street of your home town — having grown up with everyone you meet — to find people averting their eyes, turning their backs, pulling their children away from you. The Romans punished in much the same way, by banishing citizens from their beloved city. So we've long known that rejection is one of the most powerful and effective of punishments. We are social animals, and being forcibly separated from society is terribly painful.

I don't want to be hurt by the people I care about. I don't even want to be hurt by chance acquaintances! So I've spent a lifetime building little defenses, emotional walls to protect myself from rejection, criticism and disapproval. The stronger my defenses become, the more they protect me from hurt, but they also destroy any chance for real intimacy. So long as I remain aloof and self-protective, I lose out on the possibility for deep friendship, settling instead for surface relationships. Pretending not to care is self-protective, all right. It's also unloving. When I separate myself from people, I'm doing a good job of punishing myself!

I'm certain that the opposite of love is *not* hate. Isn't hate a powerful emotion, as passionate in its own way as love is? Love and hate are extraordinarily similar; we even talk of "love-hate relationships," in which two people focus enormous amounts of positive *and* negative energy on each other. I can deal with hate, because at least I know I matter! What I can't stand is apathy.

The opposite of love is indifference. Once I finally understood that, I promised myself that I would never again use the ''silent treatment'' on someone I love. If I care, I need to communicate my hurt and anger; I had better not stay withdrawn for very long. Indifference is a punishment; it's painful in a heart-wrenching, lonely way. I know I don't want to be rejected, and I don't want to punish someone who's important to me. Maybe we need a ''cooling off'' period, but after that I want to start talking!

NOTES ___________________________

COMPLIMENTS ARE ALWAYS WELCOME

THE 72nd DAY

Compliments come in three categories: from you to me, from me to you, and from me to me. I once avoided them all like the plague. You know how it goes: someone says, "How nice you look today!" and I must joke off a reply: "You mean, yesterday I didn't? Ha! Ha!" Or I brush off a remark about my choice of clothes with "Oh, this old thing!" When I squash a compliment flat, I'm not alone in being unkind to myself and the giver. Dodging, avoiding and minimizing compliments is epidemic. Shall I begin a list of all the psychological reasons for doing such a thing? My self-esteem is low, I'm embarrassed, I don't want to appear too proud, it's just a humble (!) habit, and so on. But I must quit excusing, explaining and rationalizing, because I'm putting my energies in the wrong place.

And yet . . . my mind is so used to explaining behaviors that, as I write, I hark back to my childhood — to the way my parents and teachers spoke to me. Good heavens, who cares? That's all past history, and knowing *why* I don't handle compliments well won't accomplish a thing. The fact is, I don't like the way I've dealt with them, so I've simply decided to change my behavior. I began by saying "Thank you" with a smile. Then I bit my tongue so nothing could slip out to negate what I'd just said. Eventually I was able to add little, truthful comments like, "I appreciate that," or "What a nice thing to say," or even, "You've made my day!" Now I love getting compliments, because I'm certain I won't dump on them the moment they're voiced. Curious how quickly my self-esteem has risen.

I used to feel awkward about giving compliments, even though I wanted to. Was I afraid of rejection, of being thought dishonest or self-serving? Again, no matter. Change the behavior! My criteria are simple: be sure the compliment is true, given freely and without expectations. As I've become more aware of others' unique qualities, my compliments have become more lavish and spontaneous. "Wow, do you look terrific!" makes me feel marvelous when I say it, and I get another boost when my friend lights up with pleasure.

I've finally gotten around to complimenting myself, too. Who knows better than I when I'm doing well? Aren't I allowed to give my own self a good feeling? Now that I'm more certain that I'll tell myself the truth, the self-critical and complimentary voices within me have blended. When I tell myself "That's great!" I know it really is.

Have you ever stopped to think that an honest compliment is an almost perfect gift? The price is right, it always fits, and it feels great when you put it on. A compliment never tarnishes or needs fixing, and the warehouse never runs out. I've just about forgotten how I used to squirm and minimize a compliment's positive power, now that I realize that giving and receiving them is warm, welcome and wonderful!

SPEAK "I"

THE 73rd DAY

As a child, I was taught not to say "I," because it would have been considered boastful. I was not to talk about accomplishments or material acquisitions, but it was always proper to talk about a fine film or a well-written book. (What in heaven's name do you say after you remark that you've just finished reading *Jane Eyre*?) At the same time, I was to keep up a positive self-image, underlined by the message, "Everything is fine, thank you. Just fine." I was living a lie, and had no way of knowing it. All I knew was I couldn't make smalltalk and always felt miserably uncomfortable around people. No wonder!

Here I am, a half-century later, just beginning to talk about the "inner me." I now know I'm sharing instead of boasting, and am likely to start any sentence with "I am," "I feel," "I believe," "I think," and even "I want." It's all so new, but when I talk about myself honestly, I don't get into trouble; it's the one thing I really know about. Now you're a little more likely to get the truth from me, rather than "Fine," even when it shows me in a less-than-perfect light!

When we're together, I'll be listening to you and identifying with you. That's new for me too, because my mind used to race ahead to think of some brilliant and impressive response. Now I'd rather you were comfortable with me instead of impressed, so I'm throwing out that foolish image, too. The more I share the imperfect sides of me, the better I feel. I'm no longer trying to overpower you. What a relief!

There's an old saying:

> Big people talk about ideas;
> Ordinary people talk about themselves;
> Little people talk about other people.

So here I am, an ordinary person sharing my humanity with you at last. I'm even willing to say something vulnerable like, "I feel so good talking with you." I'm laying myself open for rejection, but when your eyes light up I know we've connected somehow. I'm never going back (for any length of time) to my phony image, I promise!

NOTES

I Come First

THE 74th DAY

Often I must choose what's good for me *over* what's good for someone else. Bluntly put, *my needs absolutely must come first!* This is a hundred-and-eighty-degree turn from the way I was brought up: "Good girls" think about everyone else first, never say "I want," don't ever hurt another's feelings and are *never* angry or selfish. I was even reminded not to take the last piece of food from the serving plate. It didn't take long for these rules to translate in my head like this:

> What other people think is of the utmost importance.
> Don't be honest, just be polite.
> What I need doesn't matter; I'm not important.

Maybe "Don't be selfish" is a woman's issue. Do you ever remember anyone accusing a boy — or a man — of being merely selfish? He's just being practical or hard-headed or looking after his own interests. Well, I'm simply being practical and hard-headed and looking after my interests, too! But instead of calling it "selfish," since that word continues to have bad-girl overtones for me, I'm going to call my newfound attitude *enlightened self-interest*. I like the sound of it.

I subscribe to the idea of being a "selfless" person: able to give whenever there's a real need — nursing the ill, sitting up with a friend or stranger, filling sandbags during a flood. I'll do whatever is required to become a selfless instrument of God's will. But I'm equally certain that I can only become selfless if I remain totally selfish, protecting my mental, physical and emotional health *above all else,* so that my self-esteem and self-worth are high and whole. No, this isn't a paradoxical attitude; I must treat myself the way a mechanic treats an ambulance that's on call day and night. It must be in top condition to do its job. It doesn't get used if its oil is low; it gets oil. It doesn't get driven if its engine is rough; it gets a tune-up. Otherwise it'll be stuck in the parking lot unable to function when it's needed in an emergency. That's me, too!

This book is chock-full of self-loving concepts. I know people who complain bitterly about the present "me first" generation. I'm certainly talking "me first," but not "Gimme, gimme." Quite the opposite:

> *Me first* — so that I maintain good health and a clear head in a crisis.
>
> *Me first* — so I'm not used or abused.
>
> *Me first* — so that I can help someone selflessly.

It *does* make sense!

NOTES

Compromise Situations, Not Self

The 75th Day

It's the *little* putdowns and insults that chip away at me until my self-esteem is in the pits. Maybe it's because I also brush them away as unimportant. Let me give you an example: I'm watching some second-rate program on TV when my housemate barges in, flips off my program and settles down to watch the ball game, completely ignoring my presence. I get a flash of anger. "How dare he?" I begin to think to myself. Just as quickly, I begin a philosophical discussion in my head. "Oh, calm down. You're being too petty. My program wasn't very good, and I really don't mind watching a ball game once in a while. *How important is it, anyway?*"

Very damned important, that's how! I just got my self-worth stepped on, I was treated like a non-person with no rights — and I'm talking myself into believing it's okay! That's sick! I'd like to erase "How important is it?" from the language because it's so often misused. I'd replace it with, "How important am *I*?" I need to speak up immediately: "I'd like to be asked if I'm willing to switch channels." If he starts to argue, I simply need to repeat firmly, "I expect you to ask me first." I must remember, too, that "I don't mind" is *not* the automatic answer once he comments sarcastically, "Do you *mind*?" The answer may very well be, "Yes, I *do*!"

There are two categories of compromise. The TV putdown is an example of *self*-compromise; the other kind is *situational*. They are frequently confused. If I truly understand the difference, I can more effectively protect my integrity and self-esteem. The idea is to avoid being a doormat, while remaining flexible in social situations.

Let's say that my housemate and I are planning to go out

for dinner. I'm looking for elegant dining; he wants that cheap tavern with the "great French fries." We can make a *situational* compromise by negotiating a third location that's between the two extremes. On the other hand, if he says "No tavern, no dinner" and I'm revolted by the crummy joint, then the game has been changed. If I say yes, I'm compromising myself and my values. At this point I can say, "No thanks, I'll have dinner with Mary instead." Off I go to pick up another dinner partner, because my self-respect is important to me. Dinner with my girlfriend is great, and the next time the issue comes up, my housemate will be interested in an adult situational compromise instead of an ultimatum. I can count on it.

NOTES

An Adult Doesn't Need To Explain

The 76th Day

Many times in my life I've been vehemently accused of something:

> "You didn't do what you promised!"
> "You left this place a mess!"
> "You're out all the time!"
> "You didn't call; you didn't write!"
> "You didn't do what I told you to!"
> "You broke it!"

And I've found myself reacting to the accusatory tone of voice instead of responding to the facts. I've dredged up every apologetic excuse and rationalization I could muster, defending myself, my motives, my actions and inactions. "I didn't mean; I'm sorry; I forgot; I meant to; I didn't expect; If you'd had a week like mine . . ." Wait a minute. What am I doing? Preparing to defend myself against the truth? Now, that's patently absurd!

At last I discovered another way, a principle that was not so obvious when I was protecting my almighty self-image: *When in doubt, be honest*. Now that I'm becoming an honest adult, I no longer need a defense. An adult accepts the truth and doesn't need to explain, so I can answer simply, "You're right, I didn't," or "Yes, I did," or "That's true." Nothing else is necessary. Boy, does it stop an incipient battle cold. Who can argue with an admission of the truth?

The other side becomes equally simple. Falsely accused, I answer, "That is not true," and then I'm silent. No more need be said. (It should be obvious that these are social and family situtations I'm describing, not court-of-law problems. If you're in that kind of bind, you need legal representation and witnesses!) In relationships, if I'm consistently honest, then I've gained credibility and trust; what I say is accepted at face value. This has taken a while, but the result is that my defensive anger and outrage have melted into thin air.

NOTES

THE 77th DAY

Is some relative forever putting you down, ''shoulding'' on you, laying guilt trips on you that make you feel inadequate? Does it reduce you to helpless rage? You're not alone. Imagine the mother-in-law whose first action upon entering her son's house was to march to the kitchen and open the oven to inspect its cleanliness. Her daughter-in-law could feel her self-esteem slip and her gorge rise the moment that woman stepped onto her sidewalk! Your ogre's behavior may be more subtle, but the results are always predictable: the relative plays out the ritual and you churn inside. Every visit is *deja vu*. And that's where ''Petty Points'' comes in. I invented the game myself, and several people have played it to their advantage.

Petty Points gives you a chance to detach emotionally and to focus more objectively on the dynamics of the relationship. The game is simplicity itself. Whenever the offending person begins the characteristic litany, you keep score in your head: one point for each negative question or put-down or ''should'' that you've predicted accurately. Ten points wins the game for you. Or you can guess how many ''shoulds'' will be dumped on you in a ten-minute period. Give yourself a hundred-point bonus for an accurate prediction.

There's an important real-life bonus too. Your anxiety, anger and guilt lessen when you're able to focus on your relative's behavior rather than your own emotional reactions. Are you seeing the humor of the game? Once you're in better control, you may be able to come out with an honest, adult statement or two, opening up real lines of communication for the first time.

And what about the daughter-in-law and the Oven Inspector? She'd already won the hundred-point bonus playing Petty Points. It was time for direct action. She practiced the following statement beforehand: "I feel very inadequate when you check my stove to see if it's clean. I don't want you to do that any more." The mother-in-law was apologetic and tearful, assuring the younger woman she didn't give a hoot about her stove. The older woman simply considered her the most talented cook she'd ever known, and proudly told her friends what marvelous things she always discovered in that oven! She'd wanted to ask for recipes, but was afraid she'd be ridiculed for asking, since her own cooking was only so-so.

You, too, may discover a real person beneath all that intimidation once you stop silently accepting the same old game and play by the new rule called "honesty."

HOW DO I TAKE CARE OF MYSELF?

NEVER ASK "YOU" QUESTIONS

THE 78th DAY

Whenever someone begins to question me, I get uneasy. I become the focus of attention, but not the kind I welcome. Even when the questioning is positive and friendly, my heart beats faster and I tense up, preparing to explain and justify myself. It's like that long-ago time when the teacher pressed me with a question in the classroom, and I hadn't even read the assignment! It seems like an adversarial position: you against me. At its worst it can become a hammering, yammering assault, the very opposite of communication:

> "Don't you realize . . . ?"
> "Why don't you . . . ?"
> "Why haven't you . . . ?"
> "What are you . . . ?"
> "How can you . . . ?"
> "Can't you see that . . . ?"

Now those aren't friendly questions. They're simple accusations, to which the questioner obviously expects abject apologies, not answers! After this barrage, the funny thing is that the inquisitor is apt to lament, "He won't communicate with me." Are you serious? Who wants to stay in the war zone?

To reduce defensiveness and tension, I use a simple technique that's better for both parties. Gentler and less accusatory, it gives the other person a chance to think calmly — or not to answer at all. If the interchange is less highly charged, honest communication is more likely to result. The technique? *Never ask questions; make statements.* Simple comments like "I wondered if . . .", "I expect you to let me know when . . ."; "I was upset by . . .", all feel better to the receiver. Experiment with a friend and learn which technique works better. Those "you" questions conjure up an irate parent admonishing a rebellious, unthinking child, whereas statements are perceived as adult-to-adult communication. And that's what I really want.

NOTES

THERE ARE NO-MIND READERS

THE 79th DAY

I couldn't possibly count the number of times I've been hurt and frustrated and angrily thought to myself:

"He should've known . . ."
"She knew that I wanted . . ."
"He knows how I feel about . . ."
"I shouldn't have to tell her . . ."

as if everyone in town kept an exhaustive mental file devoted to my every whim and attitude. And when someone dares to pull the very same thing on me, do I ever get self-righteous!

"How could *I* know?"
"You never *told* me!"
"Do you think I'm a *mind-reader*?"

And the old, silent game of "If You Cared Enough You'd Know Without My Telling You" is played to its inevitable conclusion; everyone feels miserable, unloved and misunderstood. And we *are* misunderstood! How could it be otherwise, when we haven't let the other person know what's happening inside of us?

When was the last time you, as an adult, got exactly what you wanted for your birthday? I thought so. Did you *tell* anyone your heart's desire? Did you specify? "I want that green wool tweed jacket in a size twelve." Or did you ever say:

"I don't want to spend Christmas with them."
"I want my vacation at the shore this year."
"I want a hug."

I'm no longer willing to cop out with "You know how I feel" after giving you the silent treatment. I plan to be accountable for my own communication. I may even have to repeat myself. I no longer believe that pouting, silence, slamming the door or rattling the pots and pans is going to get me somewhere. It's not where I want to go! Who needs the negative attention? I've promised myself I'll let you know how I feel, what I think, what I want — what I need. It's difficult to do. If all this communication stuff were easy, I'd be better at it by now!

NOTES ______________________

CHECK YOUR MOTIVES

THE 80th DAY

Some years ago I agreed to be the chairperson for an enormous fund-raising effort that included door-to-door canvassing throughout my home town. It was a worthy cause that needed doing, but not by me! I was caring for three young children and drinking alcoholically, so you'll understand that disaster was inevitable. Oh, I handled the project just fine, increasing contributions so much they wanted me back the following year. The debacle was at home; everyone suffered. I thought I was doing a "good deed," volunteering my time to the needy. What went wrong? The fact is, I took on the project to *look* good. Later I realized that wasn't an adequate motive, but I didn't know it at the time. I didn't know much! I simply bounced from crisis to crisis trying to mold myself into something I wasn't, wondering between times why my life was so often miserable and pointless.

Now I know that reviewing my motives is necessary and helpful, though often painful. When I first began, there was no honesty in me — thanks to my carefully tended image as "good, altruistic" person. But I've persevered, rather than endlessly defending my psyche, and have become gradually more truthful. I'm realistic enough to know that motives are seldom "pure." They're usually an intermingling of attitudes, the "good" motives conveniently overshadowing any underlying pettiness, because the human mind is cunning and devious.

What are my motives?

> To protect my self-image? (Good girl, macho man)
> To put myself *above* someone else?

To control people, places and things?
To feed my greed, lust, power or revenge?
To put myself *down*?
To respond to my guilt or fear?
To run from reality or responsibility?
To support my view of myself as "victim"?
To have it *right now*, regardless?
To protect myself from rejection?
To assauge my anger? (A demand to do it *my* way)
To "buy" affection or admiration?
To prove myself right (and you wrong) at any cost?
To feed my addiction or compulsion?
To provide basic needs for food, shelter, security, love or creativity?
To express myself openly and honestly?
To do what's right, necessary and important to do (without harming myself)?

These motives can overlap. You may be able to add several more goodies. The fact is, soul-searching is uncomfortable! To become more honest about my motives, I'm learning to "relax into the truth." I'm not certain I'll ever be able to explain this any better, but I believe my daily meditation has helped. The "relaxing" attitude seems to get past my defenses and false image, and I'm more able to accept unpleasant truths about myself. Sometimes I can laugh happily at the gyrations of my mind, and confront myself with humor, shouting "Cut! This is *not* the way to go!"

What makes me continue this disconcerting journey? It has something to do with accepting the positive flow of my life. The more self-satisfying my motives, the more successful my life becomes. I measure "success" in a very different way now: *by the degree of inner peace.*

LISTEN ONLY TO THE ACTION

THE 81st DAY

We flood our minds with words! They mesmerize and manipulate us, masking the truth even when it's set down squarely in front of us. To discover the underlying reality, I've learned to *listen only to the action*. This skill took time to master, because I had to blot out the barrage of meaningless words in order to concentrate on what was *happening* rather than what was *said*.

Example One: The parents of a young man were distraught. They had agreed to care for his huge German shepherd — which had wrecked the lawn, the screen door, the carpets, the garden and their relationship with their neighbors. They wanted the monster out of their lives, but believed it wasn't their dog to give away. They wanted advice on how to get their son to find a home for the animal. How long have they had the mutt? Fourteen months!

Reality: The boy found a home for his pet fourteen months ago. The dog belongs to the parents!

Example Two: The alcoholic mother of two rambunctious teenage boys has been sober over two years. Filing for divorce, she's been assured by her lawyer that she'll get custody of the children, plus the pretentious house and sufficient cash to live comfortably. All that's required of her is that she not drink. She tells everyone that her only joy and desire in life is to have her two wonderful boys with her. That very night, after the trip to the attorney's, she got stinking drunk.

Reality: She never wanted to care for those two difficult boys and that enormous house. Let Daddy do it! (And he did.)

Example Three: "He's going to get a divorce and marry me." "Has he filed the papers yet?" "No, he's waiting for his wife to do it." "How long has he been promising you he'd get free?" "Two years."

Reality: There's no marriage in this woman's future!

Example Four: "I'm really excited. We're going to buy a house in the country." "How much of the down payment have you saved?" "Well, we had quite a bit, but we had to buy a new car and my husband decided to pay cash."

Reality: There's no house in this couple's future.

Example Five: "He wants so desperately to get well and get back to work. He hates lying around the house. It's just that he keeps forgetting to take his medicine, so it's taking him a long time to get well."

Reality: What work?

When I put down these examples, my immediate reaction is, "Of course! That's so obvious; *why don't they see it?*" But when it comes to my own life, it's not all that clear. I'm listening to people I want to trust, and probably I'm wishfully projecting a certain outcome. I want to believe the fantasy, too! I get a hint that something's wrong when I feel helpless, confused and frustrated. I know it's time to step back and analyze my situation, observing the action — or lack of it. The trick is to blow away the smokescreen of plans and promises to get at the underlying reality. I may not like what I see, but once I recognize the facts, I can begin to deal with them. My wheel-spinning dream world is gone.

There Is No Hope

The 82nd Day

If I clearly understand that my "hopes" are mere *wishful thinking*, my life probably won't get too bogged down. But I've often mislabeled my fantasies as "hopes," or used the concept as an excuse for inactivity. "I hope" can be a way to look good and sound positive while being irresponsible. It's a great way to get off the hook, because I'm really thinking: "This situation could go either way; maybe it'll go the way I want it to, and if so I won't have to take a risk right now and do something about it. I can wait and 'hope'."

I've come to understand that what I "hope for" is going to become either factually true or false; I'm living in fantasy or reality — and I'm basing my present actions on one or the other. No in between! It doesn't take long to realize that "hope" and "try" are cousins:

> TRY: You either *do* or you *don't*;
> HOPE: It either *will* or it *won't!*

The wife of an alcoholic does nothing positive about living with his drinking for twenty years. "I stay because I always have hope that he'll get better." What she actually has is an alcoholic marriage and a paralyzed attitude, which she's labeled "hope" so she can live with her personal irresponsibility.

A dying man and his family keep "hoping" he'll get better. Not only are they living in fantasy, but they're losing out on the precious, healing experience of open communication: serious talks about love, death and loss which might be spiritually uplifting for everyone. Besides, he fails to put his business affairs in order, which would be a satisfying completion for him. Everyone's pretending, and everyone loses.

Or, I've had a good job interview, and now I'm goofing off at my present job, being a second-rate employee — or just sitting around the house "hoping." I'm behaving unrealistically (I don't have the new job yet) rather than taking responsibility for my present job — or making positive use of the day by sending out more résumés and making phone calls.

How do I get away from this pointless (hopeless) point of view? I can ask myself these three questions:

1. Is my attitude, which I call "hope," keeping me from seeing the objective truth of a situation?
2. Is it preventing me from acting on the present, available facts?
3. Is it really a paralysis of irresponsibility? What are my motives for not risking or taking positive action?

The very antithesis of "hope" is positive, productive action — or simple acceptance. God grant me the wisdom to know the difference!

Either Way Is Okay

The 83rd Day

Slogans and sayings have their uses when I'm caught up in the storm of tragedy or crisis and my ego's in the midst of it. I need to take an emotional breath, step back and remind myself Who's actually in charge of my life. My daughter tells me she used to be puzzled by some of my remarks because they sounded like indifference in time of acute sadness:

It doesn't make any difference.
It either will or it won't.
It doesn't matter.
It's not important.
Either way is okay.

I'm not saying that some experiences aren't agonizing; far from it. I hurt just as much as anyone else. And I'm not advocating a hard-shell, fatalistic attitude. These expressions simply remind me that H.P.'s decisions prevail. Life unfolds the way He wishes it, according to His plan. Through these sayings, I'm acknowledging that if it doesn't go my way, it's nevertheless acceptable.

I have never had a passive, watch-life-go-by attitude. H.P. and I each have detailed job descriptions. Mine is to use *all* my God-given talents to the very best of my ability in order to accomplish His will for me, and His covers everything else. This is charmingly described in the story of the gardener. An old man has brought forth a resplendent garden after months of digging, planting and cultivating in what was once a rocky city lot. A pious woman stops to admire the glorious display. "What magnificent beauty God has created here," she remarks in admiration. "Yep," answers the tired but satisfied gardener, "but you should've seen the place when He had it by Himself."

So I do the weeding and planting and fertilizing. Whether the seeds germinate, the sun shines, the rain falls or the frost comes early are evidently not up to me. I may not get a garden this year. This may be the year of loss and separation and drought. Either way is okay.

There Are No Coincidences

The 84th Day

I don't think it's possible to waffle on this spiritual axiom. You either believe in it wholeheartedly, or you don't. Over a period of years I've travelled from total disbelief to wide-eyed wonder, coming to see that *all* the seemingly mundane events of my world are Master-minded. I now view accidents of "chance" as planned and premeditated *gifts* that I'm free to accept or reject. When I accept them, my life immediately lifts to unexpected levels. Such "coincidences" are not to be confused with premonitions, which are supposedly peeks into the future. Usually I consider them superstitious and suspect.

A few years ago, an alcoholic woman with several years of sobriety moved to a distant state. We weren't close enough to keep in touch, so she slipped easily from my mind as I went about my normally hectic daily life. Suddenly one day she flashed through my thoughts several times. I had already begun to understand that there are no coincidences, and I knew I must act quickly, or the urgent reason for her coming to mind would disappear. Timing in response to "coincidences" is of the utmost importance.

Phoning her that day, I found her drunk and suicidal. She was greatly relieved that I'd reached out to her, considering it a sign that she must do as I suggested. She unhesitatingly agreed to enter the prestigious Midwestern treatment center I recommended. (I conveniently forgot to tell her that it was always full and there might be several days' wait, because I didn't believe she'd hang around that long!) Up until that moment, her husband told me later, she'd steadfastly refused all treatment. She herself has since told me that if I hadn't called from "back home" she wouldn't have gone.

Admissions was pleased to inform me there'd just been a cancellation. Could she be there before the office closed? You bet she could! (I had no idea about distances or schedules, but I was ready to promise anything!) Her desperate husband was nonplussed when I told him what he must do. He was sprinting toward his car as his secretary made plane reservations, and within two hours husband and wife were in the air and on their way to recovery. The whole process up to flight time took me less than an hour from the moment I first paid attention to the "coincidental" fact that this woman had abruptly reappeared in my mind. Haven't you heard it said that "coincidences are God's way of remaining anonymous"?

That's just one example of a life-saving, death-diverting coincidence. They come in all sizes, bursting upon my life — and yours, too — with great consistency, transforming lives in an *instant*. Are you skeptical? I certainly used to be. I can only suggest that you do as I have: observe surprising coincidences and respond to them immediately, as I did in calling that forgotten friend. Take time to acknowledge any new direction your life may be taking as a result. Are these mere accidents of probability, or do you get a hint of Divine purpose despite your doubt?

I had to be shown over and over before I believed, but now I can accept supposed coincidences as gifts of abundance. If I reach out to embrace them, my life is instantly transformed and I'm spiritually lifted, as if I'd literally been placed in the palm of God's hand. The experience is beyond words, and at the same time it's all so common and ordinary. That's the wonder of it.

DO I ACCEPT REALITY, AND AM I OPEN TO HONESTY?

If All Else Fails, Tell The Truth

The 85th Day

A friend who came to me for advice was deeply distressed. "Every year my husband practically *commands* me to attend a party given by his boss," she explained. "It's a drunken brawl, and the host always gets crude and boorish. I absolutely hate going! Besides, it's a long evening and a far distance and I must be at work by seven the next morning. I really don't want to go. Whatever can I tell my husband?" "I have the perfect words," I assured her. "Just listen." Then I repeated practically verbatim what she'd just told me: "It's a drunken brawl; the host is crude and boorish; I absolutely hate going." When she realized what I was doing, she looked at me in astonishment. "Can I really say that?" she exclaimed. "Is it the truth?" I inquired. "Oh, yes!" was her emphatic reply.

The fact is, my friend had been asking a far different question: "*What kind of acceptable lie can I tell my husband?*" It started me thinking. How often do I lie instead of telling the truth? Am I still *living* a lie? I know each person sees a different truth, depending on upbringing, needs, beliefs and prejudices, but isn't there an objective reality beneath all the personal foggery of self-image and socialization? If honesty is the ability to perceive reality, how close am I? Isn't honesty just like sobriety and pregnancy? Then there's no such thing as being "a little bit honest"; I either am, or I'm not. (Yes, I'm aware there are many, many levels of truth; let's not get too philosophical in one short essay!)

Many of the concepts in this book deal with personally dishonest or unrealistic behaviors. In some way each one is defensive or protective, keeping me from "hurting" someone else or myself. Looking them over, I was stunned to discover how many socially acceptable ways there are to avoid reality.* Here are some of the more immediately obvious ones:

- Telling partial truths (lies) so I won't hurt someone's feelings.
- Not living in the reality of the present (one day at a time).
- Saying one thing but doing another, or not following through.
- Denying a painful reality.
- Blaming others for my behavior or the consequences of my own acts.
- Using unrealistic or dishonest words like "try," "hope," and "can't."
- Presenting an image of who I'd *like* to be rather than who I am.
- Saying yes (or no) when I want to say the opposite.
- Putting myself down, below my true worth (low self-esteem).
- Presenting an arrogant ego, above my true talents or characteristics.
- Being so self-centered I'm unable to recognize objective truth.
- Refusing to listen to or accept the validity of another's opposing view.
- Allowing others to believe a lie is truth because of my silence, people-pleasing or fear.

Notice I'm staying away from the motives of greed and power that result in thievery or fraud. I'm just recounting everyday, personally self-protective behaviors. I can no longer hang on to the image of Basically Honest Person, since these behaviors are all true of me. And yet, the very instant I admit to my dishonesty, I become honest! (As you see in these essays, I'm continually hunting for methods to chip away at dishonesty and unreality, so I'll give myself credit for personal growth too.)

---

*For you philosophers: if it's socially acceptable to avoid reality, are we a psychotic society? I've heard it said we're all more or less psychotic until about age thirty. A dandy topic for debate!

When people argue that being too honest is cruel and brutal, they're merely arguing for continued dishonesty. I don't believe cruelty is an issue unless it's the *motive* of the person expounding it. And anyway, I'm limiting this discussion to *self*-honesty — feelings, standards and values that are reports about *me*, not abut you. The cold, hard fact is that *the truth is often painful*, especially if I've been using all my self-deceptive mental footwork to avoid dealing with reality. Another fact is equally germane: *the truth will set me free*. I'm no longer trapped within my defensive walls once I'm willing to accept that first shock of honesty.

Some of my friends have become so personally honest with me that I've had glimpses of the real, vulnerable person underneath. They've even had glimmers of the real me, as I've shed tiny pieces of my protective self-image. When that honesty flashes between us, I immediately choke up and my eyes fill with tears. I feel such kinship and affirming love! It's so glorious that I can't wait to run from it and rebuild my protective walls. What's going on? Is honesty the same as intimacy? Am I really afraid to lay open the tender core of my being? Yes, I am. That's the truth.

Do I mean what the title of this essay says? Of course not! The reality is this:

Because all else fails, I must search for the truth.

All this soul-searching carries me toward increased self-awareness. Being aware of my dishonesty, I *do* become more honest. Friends have even heard me correcting myself in mid-sentence: "Wait a minute! I take that back. It's not true. What I *mean* to say is . . ." So it's a continuing journey into new ways of thinking, feeling, believing — *acting*.

NOTES

Personal Power

The 86th Day

When I was growing up, my parents didn't teach me about personal power. They were more concerned with social conformity. They wanted me to be ungreedy, unselfish and undemanding, so my early life was spent learning all those subtle methods of manipulation trained into little girls as a *substitute* for personal power. I could get what I needed while maintaining the appearance of ignoring self.

When I became a wife and mother I took effortlessly to controlling, because it felt like power. (Since we *do* have real power over very small children, we women in particular may get a false sense of power over others. For that reason we may even fail to let go of our children in slow, appropriate stages. But if we don't let go, they'll never learn self-responsibility.) At any rate, I continued to believe in my ability to control, and it spilled over into every corner of my life. Every effort was focused away from myself. Let me state that more precisely: every effort was focused away from my *self.*

Trying to control my environment made me believe I had power, but the truth is that I'm powerless over others, so I felt frustrated and impotent (which simply means powerless). Personal power is paradoxical. *I gain power only when I understand that I'm powerless* — over everything but myself. Personal power is achieved by taking personal action. In fact, if you follow the actions described in each essay of this book, you'll experience the same phenomenon. Perhaps you, too, have been looking for power in all the wrong places.

Personal power nurtures the very core of my mental, physical, emotional and spiritual being. A friend calls this core the "prime self," that center which is without doubts, hang-ups and dependencies. It's that purely good person who I believe is buried deep within each of us, under the lies and hurt, the greed, pride and defenses of self-image. The experience of personal power is open to every one of us, disguised as simple activities like learning to say "no." Once you discover how to achieve it, you want to pass the experience on.

A friend who has found her personal power puts it this way: "I feel larger inside." That doesn't sound like much when you read it, does it? You'd have to witness her transformation to understand the splendor of it. Everything about her has changed: voice, bearing, thinking, attitude. Her self-esteem is high; *she thinks highly of herself because she's become powerful*. It's not just in her head. Well, it *is* in her head, because that's where the phenomenon occurs, but it's not imaginary.

If you observe your friends, you know who has personal power. Some people glide through life, embracing it wholeheartedly and joyously; others just muddle through, heaving heavy sighs of burden and trouble. Personal-power people have troubles, too, but they don't like to waste their energy, so they don't sigh. They put their efforts into moving what they can, which is themselves.

A Lonely Place To Be

The 87th Day

If you've been using some of the ideas and techniques in these essays, then you know it's not all rose petals and Maypoles. Every change is accompanied by anxiety and awkwardness. Maybe you can handle all that, but I'd better warn you that your closest associates — family members in particular — are apt to balk. Be prepared. They may undermine every attempt at assertiveness by dragging out their lion-tamer whips of disapproval: "Back, girl! Down!" Crack! "Sit! Stay! Roll over!" The familiar, predictable ways are more comfortable for them, too. If you've been a doormat all your life, it's in their interest to keep you down.

I can't promise you much applause as you continue on your journey of spirituality and personal growth. Stand up for yourself in the face of family pressure, and you may even find yourself ostracized. Later, when they realize you've found the strength to stand by your principles, they may gather around you again with new respect and admiration. But there are no guarantees!

As you continue to change, you may be surprised to discover who remains on friendly terms with you and who doesn't. The people who gravitate to this "new" you are your true friends. They're apt to be positive, independent, honest, open, accepting. You're going to like what you see. They'll be there just when you need them, because they know that becoming your own person is scary. This inward journey of personal growth is one of the last frontiers. It starts out as a very lonely place to be. It ends on a mountaintop.

NOTES

It's My Intention

THE 88th DAY

I've purposely placed this principle near the end, because it integrates so many of the ideas in this book. The other essays need to be absorbed, and accepted, before approaching "Intention," because it requires a really open mind. For me, the concept borders on the revolutionary.

First I learned to avoid asking questions of other people, because it was so likely to set up defenses and rationalizations. Then I learned to look past their words to their actions, because it's through actions that I learn the truth. Now it's time to take those two principles and turn them to the study of myself, because I'm sure to learn truths about me through *actions* and *results.* I seldom think about responsibility any more, because it's all too easy for me to weasel out of "responsible." For example, I may lightly throw out the idea that I'm responsible for my own happiness. Sure I buy that, but is the contrary true? Am I responsible for my *un*happiness? Right away I begin to waffle, becoming "half-a-victim" if you like, by setting up all kinds of tragic scenarios over which I have imperfect control. The Principle of Intention goes light-years beyond responsibility. Let me state the same idea in a more profoundly true and powerful way:

> It's my *intention* to be happy (or unhappy) *based on my behavior and based on results.*

Here's another disturbing example: the fact is I'm gaining weight; I'm getting fat. But the whole truth is more emphatic than that simple, factual statement:

"It's my intention to be *exactly* this weight, to the very ounce."

This statement is based on my behavior and on observable results — that is, my actual eating habits and the gross numbers on the scale. If it were *not* my intention, I'd be *doing something different.* Eating one less éclair for one less ounce, perhaps, or even one *more* potato. Can this miserable statement be true? Is it really my *intention?* Indeed! Intention makes clear that I'm in *precisely* the mental, physical, spiritual, emotional and financial state I've chosen to be. This idea is bludgeoning my psyche. I don't like it! It leaves the concept of mere victimhood in the dust!

Another painful example: a truck has just hit my car broadside. I was on the main road and it came out of nowhere. Not *my* fault, I tell you! If I'm beginning to accept intentionality based on results, *must* I say to myself, "I *intended* to have an accident"? Oh, no! I'm not ready for that! But if I can't accept the unvarnished truth about myself yet, maybe I can back into it gently:

1. I was outrunning my headlights (just a little!).
2. I knew the tires were bald and slippery.
3. I wasn't wearing my seat belt.
4. I was paying less than strict attention to the road, because I was having a heated discussion with my passenger.
5. I was late to begin with, feeling rushed and harried.
6. The side windows were steamed; I couldn't see well and hadn't bothered to wipe them.
7. The car was overdue for a checkup and brake adjustment.

Okay, I've admitted to all these little behaviors, but they're not really germane, are they? Maybe I'll just admit that it wasn't my intention *not* to have an accident. Oh brother, am I squirming, and do I know it!

My daughter introduced me to this profound principle when she enrolled me in a heavy-duty personal growth program. Before writing this chapter, I discussed the ideas with her at some length. I told her flat out that I could accept *behavior* as intentional, but not *results.* She was excruciatingly patient. "If that's as far as you can go, Mother, it's okay. You think it through and come to your own conclusions." Don't you hate it when people dump an issue back in your lap where it belongs?

I've continued to do mental battle with "based on results," and have come to realize that sometimes my behavior looks like one thing, but is actually another. For example, I may trot out on a job interview every single day. It looks like it's my intention to get a job, doesn't it? Based on behavior, it would seem so. Based on results, no, because I'm still jobless. I may be undermining myself every day with inappropriate interviews, a poor attitude and so on, and not know it consciously. And that's the point. "Results" gets to the stuff I can't see.

Soon I was forced to ask myself why I was expending so much psychic energy on finding a loophole. What would I do with it? Hang it around my neck in case I needed one? Damn. That's it after all: I want to be intentional when *I* want to be, and sneak off when I don't like the consequences. I'm beginning to get it. I want to be responsible only when I feel like it. I don't like to face that truth!

I've decided to think in terms of intention, behavior *and* results. And I'm going to *listen* to my actions. By that I mean I'm going to get a feel for them by observing myself and becoming aware of the subtly hidden and broader issues. Listening to my actions also means I'll take the time to tell myself the *whole* truth, by stating, "It was my intention to . . ." Then I'll ask myself what I'm learning about me. Am I becoming more aware of my motives and the consequences of my decisions? Do I understand that this whole book has been leading me to this point? I get it! I have to keep relearning the same simple, profound principles. It's up to me. My God, my whole life is *always* up to me!

NOTES

Expect Miracles

THE 89th DAY

When I wake each morning, anticipation begins to stir in me. What miracles will I witness, or be part of — or even call into being? I'm a child ready for wonders. Miracles are unexpected joys, surprising coincidences, unexplainable experiences, astonishing beauties — absolutely anything that happens in the course of my day, except that at *this* moment I'm able to recognize its special value. Miracles are by definition part of the Creator's intricate design: each breath, each leaf, each bug, each star, each mind.

As a child I groaned inwardly when my grandmother would "ooh" and "ah" over every garden. And yet, years after she died, I knew I was beginning to sound just like her. (And that's a miracle, too, because I can feel her very essence — and my mother's too — within me!) I began to suspend critical judgment. Everyday things ceased to be mundane; they were illuminated with new significance. I was beginning to acknowledge miracles. I was surrounded by them, enveloped by them, lifted ecstatically from observation to expectation! I was truly reborn — caterpillar into butterfly.

And now, miracle of miracles, I'm sometimes able to see when miracles emanate from *me.* When people respond to me as if I've given them a special gift, I know they're reacting to my love of life. Before my eyes their expressions dissolve from despair into laughter and relief. They are truly transformed, and I'm a willing instrument.

I expect miracles. That very expectation brings them to me in abundance: a myriad miracles. They are wondrous creations: the lines of a hand, power of the storm, rainbow in a prism, purr of a kitten, patina of old wood, devastation of a volcano, glow of a flame, gentle voice of a friend, rumble of thunder, moon reflected on pondwater — a touch, a hug, a taste of new-pressed cider. How can I make a list of miracles? Let me instead describe only those things that are *not* miraculous . . .

. . . Ah, now I understand.

NOTES

The Beginning

The 90th Day

I want to leave you with this disquieting thought: some time ago I was meditating by my window, only half conscious of the heavy early-morning fog beyond the bird feeder. Suddenly a tiny bird flew from the grey haze onto the perch. In that moment I knew — in the same way I "know" my name — that a tiny piece of my Higher Power had broken loose from the earth and blown in my direction. With that amazing and miraculous new understanding of the universe, my life has been transformed.

****

On the following pages you may describe any changes in your thoughts, feelings, attitudes and actions since absorbing some of these essays. Life is forever opening in wonderful, unexpected directions. As you continue your personal journey, I wish you joy and serenity.

Judy K.
The Old Stone House
September, 1986

Judith M. Knowlton

The author is a recovering alcoholic. She holds a B.A. in Psychology from Oberlin College and an M.A. in Group Process from Seton Hall University. She has been a Certified Alcoholism Counselor in New Jersey since 1975, and has been instrumental in starting several treatment programs in that state. In 1984 she created a publishing company from her late husband's corporation, QUOTIDIAN, Inc., dedicated to books on alcoholism, other addictions, and personal growth. The first two books, *Detachment* and *Enabling,* were co-authored with Rebecca D. Chaitin, who has relentlessly red-penciled and cheered on this volume of essays.

Judy is a widow with three adult children, two daughters-in-law and one granddaughter. In February of 1986 she moved into the Old Stone House, where she lives with her three cats and two peacocks. The pond is home* to a magnificent blue heron, four ducks, seven geese and thirty-four unnamed mallards.

* Ed. Note: Don't forget the little green herons, kingfishers, carp, turtles, catfish, eels and that arrogant leaping bass!

GAYLE BURNS

Gayle's keen eye for detail has allowed her to capture the essence of the author's Old Stone House and provide insight into the calm at the "eye" of Judy Knowlton's whirlwind life.

A photographer with a wide scope of interests, Gayle has photographed everything from sports to song. Last year she was knighted by the Order of Saint John of Jerusalem and she has been included in Who's Who of American Women and Who's Who in the East.

She lives in Denville, New Jersey with a starving writer and too many cats and dogs.